Scuds or Butter?

Scuds or Butter?

The Political Economy of
Arms Control in
the Middle East

Yahya M. Sadowski

The Brookings Institution
Washington, D.C.

Library of Congress Cataloging-in-Publication data:

Sadowski, Yahya M.
    Scuds or butter? : the political economy of arms control in the
Middle East / Yahya M. Sadowski.
        p.   cm.
    Includes bibliographical references and index.
    ISBN 0-8157-7663-2 (paper : alk. paper)
    1. Arab countries—Defenses—Economic aspects.   2. Arms control—
Arab countries.   3. Arab countries—National security.   4. Military
assistance, American—Arab countries.   I. Title.
HC498.9.D4S23   1992
338.4'76234'09174927—dc20   92-28969
                                                                          CIP

9 8 7 6 5 4 3 2 1
The paper used in this publication meets the minimum requirements of the
American National Standard for Information Sciences—Permanence of paper
for Printed Library Materials, ANSI Z39.48-1984

Foreword

For the past year, a team of scholars at the Brookings Institution, the Carnegie Endowment for International Peace, Harvard University, and Stanford University have been collaborating to develop a vision of international security arrangements appropriate for the post–cold war world. They have been studying how diverse programs of arms control, defensive force configuration, and collective response to aggression might be combined into an international regime based on cooperative security. In the fall of 1991 John Steinbruner and Janne Nolan, on behalf of the cooperative security project, asked Yahya Sadowski to prepare some remarks on how the recent Gulf War had influenced the prospects for arms control in the Middle East. *Scuds or Butter?* grew from this request.

In this study, Yahya Sadowski suggests that during the first half of the 1990s there will be an unusual window of opportunity for arms control in the Middle East. He believes that this opportunity arises neither from psychology or diplomacy nor from a reduction of hostilities in the region. Rather, it emerges from economic trends that compel Middle Eastern states to contemplate arms control in their search for cheaper means of obtaining national security.

Sadowski's premise is that Middle Eastern states can no longer afford the arms races of the past. Declining oil prices and economic mismanagement, coupled with growing civilian demands to divert a greater share of the national budget into economic development programs, have created fiscal pressures that will not allow them to engage in expensive arms races. Faced with the necessity of curbing their weapons purchases or even of demobilizing existing forces, local political elites have begun to view arms control proposals with greater sympathy.

Yahya M. Sadowski is a senior fellow in the Brookings Foreign Policy program. He is grateful to Janne Nolan and John Steinbruner, who guided this project from its inception, and to Abdel-Elah Khatib, Ahmad

Mango, Michel Marto, Thomas McNaugher, Wolfgang Reinicke, Yazid Sayigh, and a score of unidentified officials, who shared their expertise and answered technical questions. Ahmad Khalidi, George Lane, Susanne Lane, Hisham Milhem, William Quandt, Sayres Rudy, and Joe Stork read early drafts of the manuscript and provided valuable criticism. Marlin Dick served as research assistant and prepared several of the tables. Donna Verdier edited the manuscript; Andrew Portocarrero, with Adrianne Goins, verified it; and Max Franke prepared the index. Louise Skillings typed the manuscript and provided administrative assistance.

Brookings gratefully acknowledges the Carnegie Corporation of New York and the John D. and Catherine T. MacArthur Foundation for providing financial support for this project.

The views expressed in this book are solely those of the author and should not be ascribed to the persons or organizations acknowledged above, or to the trustees, officers, or other staff members of the Brookings Institution.

Bruce K. MacLaury
President

December 1992
Washington, D.C.

Author's Preface

In this book I argue that Middle Eastern states may be more receptive to arms control proposals during the first half of the 1990s than they have been at any time in the last few decades. This is a controversial proposition, not one readers can be expected to take on faith. In an attempt to make the argument persuasive, the study has been heavily loaded with facts, factoids, and footnotes. Yet to ensure that these details do not obscure the overall thrust of the argument, it may be useful to summarize the analysis here.

In chapter 1, I contend that American initiatives to curb the Middle East arms race have failed because they have focused on political and psychological factors. They have sought to reduce hostility among Middle Eastern states, presuming that arms control is possible only after successful conflict resolution. Here I introduce an alternative way of looking at the problem: from an economic perspective. What has made the arms race in the Middle East dangerous is not the depth of local antagonisms but the size of local arsenals. Oil revenue, not a cultural inclination to violence, is the real foundation of the arms race in the Middle East.

Chapter 2 shows that the Arab world no longer possesses the economic resources that fueled the arms races of the past. Declining oil prices, overpopulation, economic mismanagement, and foreign policy adventurism have wreaked havoc with the economies of the Middle East. Middle Eastern states have less cash, and Arab military budgets are squeezed by both rising prices and competing demands to fund economic reconstruction. These economic pressures alone will slow the pace of arms spending, with or without a reduction of hostilities in the region.

Chapter 3 indicates that this economic situation has both triggered and been reinforced by political pressures. The ability of Arab officers to lay claim to the lion's share of the state budget has been undermined by their declining prestige; they are blamed for battlefield failures, political instability, and economic torpor in the region. The influence of the officer corps has also been challenged by growing civilian demands to divert funds from military spending to economic development programs. Civilian political elites, particularly financial technocrats, have actually begun this diversion, winning key budget battles against their military colleagues.

In chapter 4, I show that interest in arms control is growing among regional elites, who view it as a means to curb the economic cost of maintaining national security. I examine three arms control proposals that have gained a following in the Arab world: first, the Egyptian proposal to ban dangerous—and expensive—weapons of mass destruction from the region; second, proposed collective security arrangements under which participating states would pool their forces for a common defense; and third, and perhaps most promising, a Jordanian plan for an "arms-for-debt" swap which would reward those states that curbed their military spending by canceling some of their burdensome foreign debt.

In chapter 5, I look at some of the obstacles to arms control in the region. I argue that Israel and Iran, whose weapons acquisitions have played an important role in triggering local arms races, are subject to the same economic constraints as the Arab states. Viewed from an economic perspective, the most pressing threat to arms control programs in the region comes from Saudi Arabia and the Gulf states. These oil-rich countries still have enough cash or credit—and U.S. cooperation—to obtain a new generation of weapons and thereby provoke a renewal of the arms race.

Together these arguments provide an alternative way of understanding what drives the Middle Eastern arms race, what measures are most likely to curb it, and who might be most interested in arms control. They do not attempt to purvey specific blueprints for arms control in the Middle East, nor do they try to anticipate what arms control agreements might actually be achieved. Instead, they show how current conditions might best be exploited to get negotiations moving and how their prospects for success might be enhanced.

Y. M. S.

Contents

1. Oil Money and Arms Races in the Middle East   1

2. The Arab Economic Crisis and the Gulf War   11
   Iraq *13*
   Jordan *17*
   Saudi Arabia *19*

3. The Politics of Arab Demilitarization   25
   Evolving Attitudes in the Officer Corps *29*
   Budget Battles in Syria *32*
   From Demilitarization to Arms Control *38*

4. Arab Arms Control Initiatives   39
   Arms Control Proposals *40*
   Jordan's Arms-for-Debt Proposal *44*
   Regional Security Proposals *51*
   What Will Work? *55*

5. Threats to Arms Control   56
   Israel *57*
   Iran *61*
   Saudi Arabia *66*
   The Possibilities for Change *72*

6. Conclusions   78

Notes   83

Index   113

Tables

1-1. Indicators of Level of Militarization, by Geographic Area, 1988   3

1-2. Deaths Caused by War, by Geographic Area, 1945–90   10

2-1. Cost of Iraq's Invasion and Occupation of Kuwait   20

2-2. Indicators of Fiscal Pressure, by Country, 1980 and 1990   22

3-1. Regional Comparison of Military and Social Expenditures, 1986   26

3-2. Human Development in Selected Arab and Developing Countries, 1992   27

3-3. Foreign Debt of the Arab States, 1990   34

4-1. Hypothetical Arms-for-Debt Swap at a 1:2 Ratio, 1987   48

4-2. Military Manpower of the Gulf Cooperation Council States and Neighbors, 1991–92   53

5-1. Countries That Drive the Arms Race in the Middle East   57

5-2. U.S. Arms Sales to the Middle East, August 2, 1990– September 14, 1992   75

Figures

1-1. Arab Petroleum Revenues and Military Spending, 1963–88   9

CHAPTER 1

Oil Money and Arms Races in the Middle East

THE 1991 GULF WAR[1] highlighted the danger that arms races in the Middle East pose to world peace. During the war, then–U.S. Secretary of State James A. Baker III observed that, with "the fourth largest army in the world . . . Iraq is not a third-rate military power. . . . Iraq has more battle tanks than the United Kingdom and France combined. It has more combat aircraft than either Germany, France, or the United Kingdom."[2] In fact, even *after* its devastating defeat by the United States, Baghdad deployed 50 percent more main battle tanks than did the United Kingdom.[3] Possessing an arsenal of this size inflated Iraqi ambitions and fueled the aggressive instincts of Saddam Hussein.

Yet Iraq is not the only third world, Middle Eastern state that has built a first world military machine. Egypt, Syria, and Israel each own more battle tanks than France and the United Kingdom combined, and, as *The Economist* reports,

> In a war Syria could field about 800,000 men with about 4,000 tanks and 550 combat aircraft. A fully mobilised Israel has armed forces of more than 500,000 men with about 4,000 tanks and 600 combat aircraft. If Egypt called up its reserves it would have more than 1m men under arms, with about the same number of tanks and aircraft as Israel. The whole Middle East, not just Iraq, is grotesquely over-armed.[4]

That these forces are bolstered by a growing number of chemical weapons and ballistic missiles, not to mention (in the case of Israel) a tidy stockpile of nuclear bombs, is clearly cause for concern.

These armories were not built in a day, and they did not come cheap. Financing the buildup called for enormous sacrifices from an already-impoverished general population. Yet for the last twenty years, the Middle East has had the dubious distinction of being the world's largest arms market: from 1979 to 1988 the region imported at least $154 billion

1

worth of weapons, and during the 1980s, about one-third (by value) of all weapons traded internationally were destined for the Middle East.[5] Indeed, of the five countries that imported the most arms during the 1980s (Iraq, Saudi Arabia, India, Syria, and Iran), only one was not in the Middle East.[6] Levels of military expenditure were higher in the Middle East—by almost any measure—than in any other region of the world (table 1-1).

If the Iraqi invasion of Kuwait alerted the world to the danger of the arms race in the Middle East, the American victory over Iraq seemed to create an opportunity for restricting the flow of arms to the region. The skill with which U.S. President George Bush was able to assemble and sustain an international coalition to reverse Iraqi aggression, the lopsided triumph of allied arms in Operation Desert Storm, and the low cost of the conflict in terms of allied lives and disruptions to Western economies bred a wave of optimism. President Bush himself insisted that the allied triumph contained the germ of a "new world order" that might transform the Middle East.[7] Other leaders too expressed a degree of optimism that had been rare since the end of World War I, claiming that the allied victory had created a climate conducive to conflict resolution, arms control, and international intervention against aggression.

In Washington, many hoped that Operation Desert Storm would produce an epiphany, a massive change of heart that would defuse the conflicts plaguing the region. They believed that the magnitude of the American victory and the Iraqi defeat would "shock the region out of its pathological political culture."[8] Columnist Jim Hoagland spoke for many when he wrote,

> It is the psychological effect of victory, rather than military prowess in battle, that could help change the Arab world. With Arab participation, the victors in this war exposed the emptiness of the radical Arab nationalist appeal mouthed by Saddam Hussein and spawned by the frustration of five decades of defeat by Israel.
>
> That spirit of defeat created paranoia and scapegoating of the West and of Israel, which paralyzed Arab politics. Saddam's defeat is an opportunity for the Arab world to rise out of this dismal swamp.[9]

If the Arabs could be freed from their "radical illusions," then perhaps their traditional hostility toward Israel and their ambivalence toward the West might diminish.

The Bush administration erected its policy toward the postwar Middle East on the premise that this epiphany should be encouraged and con-

Table 1-1. Indicators of Level of Militarization, by Geographic Area, 1988

| Area | Military expenditures | | Per capita military expenditure (dollars) | Armed forces per 1,000 population |
	Percent of central government expenditures	Percent of GNP		
Latin America	6.9	1.3	27.87	3.7
East Asia	11.0	2.0	44.76	4.7
Africa	13.6	4.2	25.28	2.9
South Asia	16.8	3.8	11.81	1.9
Europe	17.2	6.1	633.60	11.1
United States	27.5	6.3	1,250.81	9.1
Middle East	30.1	8.8	344.49	18.3

Source: U.S. Arms Control and Disarmament Agency, *World Military Expenditures and Arms Transfers, 1989* (October 1990), pp. 31–34, 69.

solidated. In a hurried series of interagency meetings in early 1991, the administration devised new policy initiatives in four areas.[10] First, it tried to renew the Arab-Israeli peace process, building on the de facto collaboration among Israel and "moderate" Arab states in the coalition. Second, it hoped to spur economic development in the region by uniting rich and poor states around a program of market-oriented growth. Third, it wanted to devise new collective security arrangements to protect the Arab Gulf states. Finally, it sought to build upon the new, higher level of international cooperation and the apparent reduction of Arab-Israeli tensions by limiting arms proliferation, particularly of weapons of mass destruction.

On May 29, 1991, in an address at the U.S. Air Force Academy in Colorado Springs, President Bush unveiled the details of an American initiative to promote arms control in the Middle East. He called for a regional freeze on the acquisition, production, and testing of surface-to-surface missiles. He advocated a ban on the production of plutonium, enriched uranium, or any other element that could be used as fissile material for nuclear weapons. He reiterated a call for an end to the production of chemical and biological weapons. Finally, he called for negotiations among major weapons-exporting countries to reduce the flow of arms to the region.[11]

The course of the following year deflated Washington's optimism. Not only did Saddam Hussein survive his defeat in Kuwait, he apparently consolidated his power within Iraq, and ordered hundreds of thousands of Kurdish and Shi'i insurgents massacred while allied troops gazed anxiously on. The hoped-for diminution of Middle Eastern hostilities failed to materialize. Richer Arabs, who had backed Kuwait, continued to feud with poorer Arabs, who tended to sympathize with Iraq. Operation Desert Storm certainly did not diminish the suspicion with which Arab leaders regarded each other—much less Israel. Only after months of American diplomacy and pressure did Israel, Syria, Jordan, and the Palestinians agree just to attend bilateral peace talks.

The bilateral negotiations quickly bogged down in rhetoric and contributed little to conflict resolution. Initially, the slow pace of the peace talks could be attributed to the stance of Israel's Shamir government, which "intended to drag out talks on Palestinian self-rule for 10 years while attempting to settle hundreds of thousands of Jews in the occupied territories."[12] But the June 1992 Israeli elections replaced Shamir with Yitzhak Rabin, who sincerely wanted to negotiate with the Arabs. Still, Rabin's enthusiasm by itself was not enough to bridge the gap between the two sides. The question of how to reconcile Israel's demands for security with Arab demands for restitution of the territories occupied since 1967 remained unanswered. The peace talks eventually showed some signs of movement, but at a glacial pace that dampened the optimism that had prevailed in Washington.

The lack of rapid progress in the peace talks also posed problems for regional arms control. Most Middle Eastern countries had applauded Bush's May initiative, but few acted on it. With prodding from the Bush administration, Israel and the Arabs had agreed to attend not only bilateral peace talks but multilateral negotiations on arms control. However, participants in the multilateral negotiations seemed to assume that the arms control talks must remain desultory until the peace talks had produced some breakthrough.[13] Partly their stance reflected a philosophical conviction that arms control would proceed more easily in the wake of progress in conflict resolution. Partly it reflected their political realization that withholding concessions on arms control could be a powerful bargaining chip in the peace talks. As a result, the multilateral arms control talks were hamstrung from the outset. Negotiators described the deliberations as unusually tepid and pedestrian; the Lebanese and the Syrians—after Israel, the most heavily armed actors in the Arab-Israeli conflict—refused to even attend.[14]

Negotiations among the major arms suppliers were equally unproductive. The "Big Five" countries that supplied most of the Middle East's weapons (the United States, the United Kingdom, France, the Soviet Union, and China) met three times, in Paris (July 1991), in London (October 1991), and in Washington (May 1992). Although they concurred that the regulation of sales to Middle Eastern combatants was urgently needed, they could not agree on practical measures to achieve that objective. Each supplier emphasized the need for controls on the weapons that the other suppliers sold. They had difficulty agreeing on a press communiqué, much less a treaty. The one concrete accomplishment to emerge from the talks was an agreement to notify each other of arms sales to the Middle East, and even this modest step provoked a rancorous debate over whether notification should be given before or after sales had been made.[15]

Gradually, the attitude in Washington toward Middle Eastern arms control shifted to one of cynical pessimism. Editorialists began to argue that, while "the aim seems noble," efforts to curb the arms trade were "doomed."[16] Richard Perle, a former assistant secretary of defense who had been a major influence on arms talks for twenty years, told Congress that efforts to control the flow of weapons to the Middle East were pointless because "wars are made by men—not the weapons with which they equip their armies—and any policy that fails to comprehend that enduring truth is certain to go wrong."[17] Perle's assertion is the foreign policy analogue of the National Rifle Association's slogan: guns don't kill people—people kill people. Perle and other authorities who argued that arms control in the Middle East was impracticable urged the United States to instead use arms sales to its allies to construct a favorable balance of power in the region. Conversely, they argued that arms control should be applied primarily to opponents of the United States and its allies. In their view, only unquestionable allies should receive arms, and

> the primary focus of US efforts in the Middle East should be those countries and groups which it does not want to see equipped with anything more than token forces. Obvious candidates include Iran, Iraq, Libya, Syria, and Yemen, as well as all terrorist groups, the Palestine Liberation Organization, and any current friends who might become hostile to US interests or who provide military support to hostile governments. Equally, the United States should be wary of multilateral control efforts that are more likely to penalize its friends than its adversaries.[18]

Those who espoused a "balance of power" argued that "objective conditions," not to mention psychological ones, made arms control impracticable in the Middle East. Undoubtedly, the region is plagued by fundamental conflicts over land, ideology, and justice. Most borders in the Middle East are recent innovations, "lines in the sand" drawn by colonial powers during this century; they remain permeable, vague, and, as often as not, hotly contested.[19] These weak borders divide radically different types of states, variously led—by secular nationalists, traditional monarchists, and Islamic revolutionaries, among others—that compete for resources and ideological influence. When these regimes are not actively at war with one another, they engage in a host of low-intensity conflicts designed to weaken and subvert their opponents. Real conflicts—not paranoia—have driven the arms race in the region. Middle Eastern governments have built up huge military machines both to intimidate their neighbors and to deter the so-called imperialist powers whose influence remains important.[20]

The arms races among these rivals have been unusually explosive because diverse local antagonisms are linked in a vicious circle. When, for instance, the Kingdom of Saudi Arabia enhances its armaments to compete with the Islamic Republic of Iran, it perhaps inadvertently triggers anxiety in Tel Aviv. When Israel responds by enhancing its own arsenal, it forces a corresponding escalation in Syria (and Jordan or Egypt). New acquisitions of weapons by the Syrian military may, in turn, provoke responses by Turkey or Iraq. And the growing power of Istanbul or Baghdad may ignite countermeasures in Iran, threatening Saudi Arabia, which sets the circle in motion again. All too often, the expansion of the military or the introduction of new weapons into *any* state in the region provokes similar escalation in all the rest. In this way, a dozen bilateral competitions spur an appalling, regionwide arms race.

Consider missile proliferation. The Soviets introduced the first Scud-B missiles to the Middle East when they sold them to Egypt in 1973, and then to Iraq and Syria in 1974.[21] Iraq was the first country in the region to use Scuds in combat, firing them at targets in Iran beginning in 1982. By 1985 the Iranians had acquired their own Scud-Bs—first from Syria and Libya, later from China and North Korea—and began retaliatory attacks against Iraq.[22] Baghdad spent billions of dollars trying to acquire a new missile or to extend the range of the Scud-B so that it could hit targets deep in Iran. The Iraqis finally developed their own longer-range Scud, the Hussein rocket. On February 29, 1988, they fired Hussein rockets at Tehran, provoking a "War of the Cities" in which Iran and Iraq launched almost two hundred missiles at each other's population centers. For Baghdad this campaign proved surprisingly effective: a quarter of Tehran's population fled the city and popular support for the war declined in Iran.[23]

The War of the Cities triggered a wave of "missile mania" that swept over the Middle East. In March 1988 Saudi Arabia, worried by its rapidly deteriorating relations with Tehran, announced that it had purchased CSS-2 missiles from China with a range of 2,700 kilometers.[24] The proliferation of missiles in the Gulf alarmed the Israelis particularly. In July 1987 Israel had test-launched its own Jericho II missile, with a projected range of 1,450 kilometers, and in September 1988 Tel Aviv pushed the missile race into outer space by launching the Shavit, a four-stage rocket that could be reconfigured as an intercontinental ballistic missile with a 7,000-kilometer range.[25] This development naturally frightened the Syrians, who started negotiations with China for the purchase of M-9 missiles with a 600-kilometer range.[26] Egypt had already joined the proliferation game in 1987 when it negotiated a deal to assist Iraq in developing a 1,000-kilometer missile, the Condor II. In the year following the first Iraqi use of the Hussein rocket, a dozen states concluded that their short-range (280-kilometer) Scud-Bs were no longer adequate and rushed to acquire longer-range missiles.

This pattern of overlapping and reinforcing antagonisms has led experts to conclude that arms control measures that have proved successful elsewhere will not work in the Middle East. For example, in central Europe arms control was possible because all the states involved were clustered in two blocs (the North Atlantic Treaty Organization [NATO] and the Warsaw Pact) that sought rough military parity and were able to negotiate through normal diplomatic channels. Things are different in the Middle East. There are no clear blocs: a country like Saudi Arabia feels threatened not only by Iran and Israel but also by Iraq and (to a lesser degree) the Yemen. There is no desire for military parity: Israeli strategic doctrine is rooted in the quest for military superiority over any combination of Arab states that might be arrayed against Tel Aviv.[27] And the options for negotiation are limited: only one Arab state has normal diplomatic relations with Israel, many have suspended relations with Iran, and virtually all have at least one Arab rival with which they refuse to communicate.[28]

The militarization of the Middle East has also been aggravated by outside powers and the logic of the international arms trade. The largest purveyors of weapons in the Middle East have consistently been the permanent members of the UN Security Council: the Soviet Union, the United States, France, China, and the United Kingdom.[29] Weapons exports from these countries have been driven partly by the desire for cash—even the richer of them view foreign arms deals as a way to reduce the unit costs of their own weapons acquisition programs. Arms sales also permit them to expand their influence in the Middle East by bolstering their local allies or at least frustrating their adversaries. Moreover, Middle Eastern regimes often buy advanced weapons systems—even when their military utility is dubious—as a way of demonstrating the strength of their ties to their superpower allies.[30]

This litany of reasons why arms sales to the Middle East are resistant to regulation contains much truth, but it is incomplete and misdirected. It overlooks the major force driving the regional arms race, and thereby misses the best hope for its restraint. One more element must be included in the litany: the economics of petroleum.

Petroleum is the key to the strategic significance of the Middle East. This region holds two-thirds of the world's proven oil reserves.[31] If the region's major export were cotton, the big powers would have little interest in selling arms to their Middle Eastern allies, let alone in deploying hundreds of thousands of troops to defend them. Moreover, without oil the Middle Eastern states could not have financed the large-scale arms imports that characterize the region. Revenue from oil exports unmistakably parallels military expenditures (see figure 1-1).

According to calculations of the Stockholm International Peace Research Institute, between 1972 and 1988 the states of the Middle East spent 11.6 percent of their gross domestic product (GDP)—more than any other region of the world—on the military. This level of expenditure would have been unimaginable without petrodollars. Even some Arab states that were not major oil exporters (Jordan, Syria, and South Yemen) spent more than 20 percent of their GDP on the military, thanks to aid and subventions from their oil-rich neighbors.[32]

Oil makes the large armories of the Middle East possible, and the outsized armories make conflicts in the region so potentially lethal. But the huge arsenals do not mean that the inhabitants of the Middle East are intrinsically more violent than those of any other region, as some "experts" have mistakenly concluded.[33] In fact, since World War II, war and civil strife have annihilated a larger share of the population in Africa and in East Asia than in the Middle East (see table 1-2).

There is, of course, real violence in the Middle East. But this is hardly surprising: violence occurs wherever poverty, social inequality, and lack of development breed despair. The same problems that breed violence

Figure 1-1. Arab Petroleum Revenues and Military Spending, 1963–88

Billions of current U.S. dollars

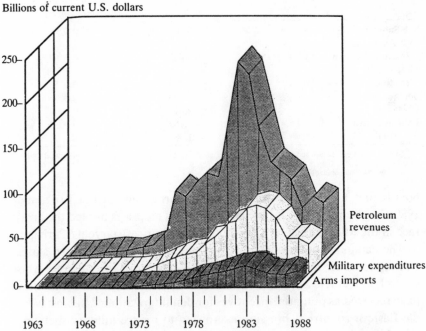

Sources: U.S. Arms Control and Disarmament Agency (ACDA), *World Military Expenditures and Arms Trade, 1963–1973* (1975), pp. 20–66, 78–123; ACDA, *World Military Expenditures and Arms Transfers, 1965–1974* (1976), pp. 19–53, 56–72; ACDA, *World Military Expenditures and Arms Transfers, 1985* (August 1985), pp. 52–88, 94–130; ACDA, *World Military Expenditures and Arms Transfers, 1989* (October 1990), pp. 36–72, 78–114; *OPEC Annual Statistical Bulletin, 1990* (Vienna: The Secretariat, Organization of Petroleum Exporting Countries, 1990), pp. 5–6; and International Monetary Fund, *International Financial Statistics Yearbook, 1991* (Washington, 1991), *passim.*

in Beirut fuel conflicts in Burma, Burundi, and Birmingham. What makes the Middle East different is the sophistication of the weapons that its inhabitants wield. And, again, oil wealth buys these sophisticated weapons. Without petrodollars, conflicts would still occur in the Middle East, but most would be resolved with hand grenades and machine guns—as they are in the Punjab—instead of advanced tactical bombers and ballistic missiles.

Surprisingly, the connection between oil exports and the arms race holds a germ of hope. Oil prices change even more rapidly and violently than governments do. Petroleum exports no longer supply the massive hard currency revenues they once did. Burdened by rapid population growth and economic mismanagement, Middle Eastern states face rapidly rising expenses that lay claim to whatever revenues remain. Squeezed between declining revenues and rising costs, the petrodollar

Table 1-2. Deaths Caused by War, by Geographic Area, 1945–90

Area	Number (millions)	Conflict deaths per 1,000 inhabitants[a]
Sub-Saharan Africa	5.207	0.0244
East Asia (excluding Japan and China)	8.083	0.0297
Middle East (including Turkey)	2.176	0.0153
South Asia	3.203	0.0056
China	2.610	0.0040
Latin America	.705	0.0033
Total	21.984	. . .

Source: Ruth Leger Sivard and others, *World Military and Social Expenditures, 1991* (Washington: World Priorities, 1991), pp. 22–25, 51–53.

a. Based on 1960 population figures.

hoards that financed the Middle Eastern arms race in the 1970s and 1980s are disappearing. If historically a rise in oil prices has fed the arms race in the Middle East, could a decline in oil prices starve it? Perhaps.

The economic crisis does not guarantee that Middle Eastern states will reduce their military spending or become more receptive to arms control. Nonetheless, economic forces deserve more attention than they have received as potential incentives for demilitarization.[34] In most Middle Eastern countries, pressure is growing to reduce military spending in order to free funds for civilian economic investment. This movement provides a more reliable and powerful foundation on which to formulate arms control initiatives than any psychological epiphany does.

CHAPTER 2

The Arab Economic Crisis and the Gulf War

THAT THE MIDDLE EAST confronts a cash shortage runs counter to the Western notion that the region is awash in oil money.[1] During the 1970s, when oil prices rose from less than $2 a barrel to nearly $40, some Middle Eastern countries and individuals became fabulously wealthy. Between 1973 and 1982 the Arab states exported more than a trillion dollars worth of petroleum products, which surpassed the value of all exports from Japan during the same period.[2] This surge of petrodollars enabled some states to build up large financial reserves; money accumulated more quickly than it could be spent.

During the 1980s, however, revenues declined while expenses continued to rise. Growing population and rising food imports forced the larger Arab states to borrow huge sums. Wars and arms races devoured much of the accumulated capital. By 1991, when Operation Desert Storm swept through the region, the Middle East had become a sea of poverty in which only a few islands of prosperity managed to remain above water.

Petroleum prices began to soften in 1982 when new oil strikes and energy conservation began to reduce the demand for imports in the industrialized countries. Members of the Organization of Petroleum Exporting Countries (OPEC) tried to adjust to declining prices by increasing the volume of their sales, but this only produced a glut that in 1985 triggered a collapse in oil prices. The value of Arab petroleum revenues dropped from $216 billion in 1980 to $54 billion in 1986 (see figure 1-1 in chapter 1).

The declining petrodollar flow affected all the Arab states. In most Arab states, oil exports made up only a small share of gross national product (GNP) or were nonexistent. Yet even those states relied heavily on petrodollars transferred from their richer neighbors in the form of

11

investment, workers' remittances, or foreign aid. Between 1980 and 1988 the two major Arab donors, Saudi Arabia and Kuwait, cut their aid funding by 64 percent and 91 percent, respectively. During the same period, aid transfers by Arab states dwindled from $8.7 billion a year to $2.3 billion a year.[3]

Despite reduced revenues, Arab governments were slow to curb their expenditures. In part, population growth engendered rising expenses. In all but two Arab states, Egypt and Tunisia, the rate of annual population increase is higher than the average for the developing countries (2 percent); in Iraq, Jordan, Libya, Oman, Qatar, Saudi Arabia, Syria, and Yemen, it is more than 3 percent.[4] The political stability of Arab regimes hinges on the ability to meet the basic economic needs of this expanding population through state programs that create employment, subsidize food prices, and give economic elites an opportunity to skim commissions from government contracts. Fearful of the political turmoil that curbing these programs might cause, the Arab states delayed painful spending cuts until the 1985 price collapse convinced them that no new petroleum boom was likely soon.

Even then, they did not curtail spending enough to offset the 75 percent drop in petroleum revenues. In 1988 the Arabs were spending $2 billion more on food imports than they had in 1980. Algeria, Jordan, Kuwait, Libya, Mauritania, Saudi Arabia, Tunisia, the United Arab Emirates, and the Yemen all imported more than half of their food needs, and Egypt was one of the world's three largest grain importers.[5]

Although the richer Arab Gulf states were able to cover the gap between what they spent and what they earned by drawing down their capital reserves, most Arabs did not possess such flush overseas accounts. They could meet their bills only by borrowing from foreign governments or commercial banks. They amassed huge volumes of debt in the early 1980s, when international interest rates were high. By 1986 the Arab states had accumulated at least $80 billion in foreign debt, which cost $11 billion dollars a year to service. Indeed, in 1989, relative to GNP, the foreign debts of Egypt, Jordan, Morocco, South Yemen, and the Sudan were larger than those of Brazil, Mexico, the Philippines, or Poland. By 1990 the World Bank had declared Egypt, Mauritania, Morocco, and the Sudan "severely indebted," and Algeria, Syria, and the Yemen "moderately indebted."[6]

Because economic growth outside the petroleum sector was negligible, borrowing only delayed the day of reckoning. By the end of the

1980s, Arab governments were besieged on two fronts. Economically, their budgets were severely constricted. The hard currency earnings of the poorer states were being exhausted by debt payments, and even the rich states began to post regular budget deficits when they could not finance their expenditures entirely from savings. Politically, the erosion of the average citizen's standard of living triggered increasingly dangerous waves of popular dissent. By 1990 all Arab leaders had cause to worry that the structure that kept them in power might crumble at any moment.

Iraq

When the political order in the Arab world began to fracture, it was no surprise that the first cracks appeared in Baghdad. Saddam Hussein's 1980 invasion of Iran triggered eight years of war which exhausted the Iraqi economy. Estimates of the military expenditures and economic damages shouldered by Iraq during the eight-year struggle range from $120 billion to $453 billion. The higher estimate exceeds the value of Iraq's oil exports since pumping began, and even the lower figure is more than the total value of Iraqi oil exports since 1973.[7] When the war ended, Saddam promised to compensate the Iraqi people by rapidly rebuilding the Iraqi economy. He budgeted $30–$35 billion for reconstruction projects, including a new Baghdad subway station, an airport in Mosul, expansion of the port at Umm Qasr, and complete rebuilding of the war-damaged cities of Basra and Fao. But to extend Baghdad's power throughout the Arab world, he dreamed also of expanding his military machine. To that end, he appropriated $5 billion a year (for 1988–92) for rearmament.[8]

A massive gap had emerged between Saddam's ambitions and his revenues, however. Even in peacetime, the Iraqi fiscal deficit ran $4–$5 billion each year. Iraq's oil exports brought the government between $13 billion and $15 billion in hard currency a year, but civilian imports alone cost $12 billion a year, including $3 billion for essential food imports. Another billion dollars a year was absorbed in paying the salaries of the million guestworkers who had replaced Iraqi workers conscripted for the military.[9] Perhaps most important, Baghdad needed around $5 billion a year to service its debts and maintain its international credit standing. To prosecute the war with Iran, Saddam had borrowed

$42 billion from Western commercial banks and Eastern bloc states and another $34–$40 billion from Saudi Arabia and Kuwait. In 1990 Iraq owed almost $90 billion in foreign debts, nearly as much as Brazil or Mexico and more than any other state in the Middle East.[10]

Saddam had counted on assistance from the oil-rich Gulf states to finance his postwar dreams. He expected them to forgive their loans to Iraq. Kuwait pointedly refused to do so. He asked them to contribute $10 billion each toward Iraq's reconstruction, but the Kuwaitis offered only $500 million spread over three years.[11] Worst of all, Kuwait and the United Arab Emirates were overpumping their OPEC export quotas. The resulting oil glut on international markets drove the price down from about $20 a barrel in January 1990 to $14 a barrel at the end of June. Each one-dollar drop in the price of a barrel of oil cost Iraq $1 billion a year in export revenue.[12] Saddam sent a series of high-level delegations to the Gulf, warning them to be more generous and reminding them of the Iraqi proverb, "Cutting necks is better than cutting the means of living."[13]

Despite Saddam's lofty rhetoric about territorial claims and Arab unity, his invasion of Kuwait was prompted almost entirely by economic desperation. He gambled that by sending his troops south he could not only wrest control of banks and oilfields from Kuwait, but pressure the other Arab Gulf states to stop overpumping their oil quotas and to deliver more aid. But Saddam's gambit backfired, triggering the 1991 Gulf War that totally disfigured his country.

During Operation Desert Storm, allied air forces dropped 88,500 tons of munitions on Iraq. Of these, only 7 percent were the much-touted "smart bombs" that produced such brilliant results in Pentagon videos. The remainder were conventional weapons that hit their targets only 25 percent of the time. Thus, 61,950 tons of munitions—70 percent of the total—missed their objectives. Nonetheless, by flying repeated sorties the U.S. Air Force was able to demolish virtually all its targeted objectives.[14]

Contrary to early press reports, the Pentagon did not narrowly target military objectives. In keeping with modern strategic doctrine, economic institutions that could help Iraq move, arm, feed, supply, and fund its troops were also demolished. Indeed, "some targets, especially late in the war, were bombed primarily to create postwar leverage over Iraq, not to influence the course of the conflict itself. Planners now say their intent was to destroy or damage valuable facilities that Baghdad could not repair without foreign assistance."[15] Thus, in addition to bombing troop concentrations, airfields, weapons plants, and telecommunications systems, the allies sought to destroy petroleum refineries and oil export terminals; factories producing glass, cement, and tires; iron and steel plants; and all electrical and mechanical industries.

The results were impressive. Of Iraq's twenty major electricity generators, eleven were totally destroyed and another six damaged. Planes showered transmission lines with metallic filaments that created short circuits and destroyed 90 percent of Iraq's electrical grid. Two of Iraq's three major oil refineries were hit by concerted bomb attacks, and production facilities at the southern oilfields of Rumaila and Zubair were badly damaged when the ground war swept over them. Virtually every phone exchange, microwave relay, and cable network was destroyed, shattering Iraq's telecommunications facilities, the most advanced element of its economic infrastructure. Roads and railroads were "rubble-ized," with special attention paid to bridges: "78 fixed span bridges, 26 pontoon bridges, [and]18 railway bridges" were destroyed or badly damaged.[16]

A UN mission sent to survey the damage in March 1991 described it as "near-apocalyptic" and noted that "now, most means of modern life support have been destroyed or rendered tenuous. Iraq has, for some time to come, been relegated to a pre-industrial age, but with all the disabilities of post-industrial dependency on an intensive use of energy and technology."[17] Repairing the physical damage would cost Iraq at least $30 billion, about half of it in hard currency, according to a classified U.S. Central Intelligence Agency (CIA) estimate.[18] Iraq's own estimates were higher: Baghdad plans to spend $20.7 billion in hard currency on reconstruction imports alone.[19]

Physical reconstruction, however, forms only a fraction of the overall cost of the war to Iraq. So long as the UN embargo remains in place, Iraq is deprived of the benefits of trade—including the revenue it derived from oil exports ($15 billion annually before the war). The United Nations has also approved plans to saddle Iraq with indemnities of at least $50 billion, to be paid partly out of Baghdad's overseas assets and partly from a tax on future oil revenues, to compensate Kuwait and other victims of Saddam's aggression.[20]

Of these various nonphysical costs, perhaps the largest is that resulting from wartime dislocations: the cost of idled plants, unemployed workers, and forgone production. Factories destroyed by bombing cannot contribute to the gross domestic product. Intact factories made inoperative by power outages or shortages of parts and raw materials create no jobs. Even if these factories were reopened, Iraq would have difficulty staffing them. Current estimates are that 177,500–243,000 Iraqis—more than half of them civilians—died during Operation Desert Storm and the Iraqi civil war that followed.[21] Moreover, these conflicts turned another 1.6 million Iraqis into refugees.[22]

The destruction of so many lives profoundly affected Iraqi production. Most experts believe that Iraq's GDP fell to a fraction of its prewar value.[23] The damage tally is hard to calculate because the cost of the war to Iraq is still growing. Injuries inflicted during the war snowballed after the cessation of hostilities. For example, power outages caused by allied bombing and shortages of spare parts caused by the UN embargo crippled Iraq's extensive agricultural irrigation system. Baghdad had hoped to harvest between 1.5 and 2.0 million tons of grain in 1991, but damage to the irrigation system reduced that figure to about 800,000 tons—only three months' supply.[24] The poor harvest created shortages of feedstock, which decimated poultry and livestock production, and forced Iraq to import seed for the following year's planting.

Shortages of agricultural goods and imports triggered a massive rise in prices. Overall inflation ran more than 250 percent during the first five months of 1991, and the cost of food rose by 1,500–2,000 percent.[25] Consequently, as reported in July 1991, "out of an average salary of 50 dinars a week, Iraqis now must pay 18 dinars for a kilo of beef, up from 14 a week ago and one dinar before the invasion of Kuwait. A kilo of flour has risen 40-fold, to 4.5 dinars. Other staples, such as chicken, have simply vanished from the market."[26] Men had to work two or three jobs and women had to sell their jewelry just to buy food. The personal savings of an entire generation of Iraqis evaporated in months.

The rise of prices and the collapse of savings grew worse over time and promised to cripple future Iraqi efforts to develop. Monies were diverted from investment to simple survival. "The consequences of war are not fully realized during the time of active conflict," one American expert noted, "and the aftermath carries with it a very real burden of death and disability."[27]

By the end of 1991 the average Iraqi family, once among the most prosperous in the Arab world, had seen its living standard fall below the poverty line, even as defined by poor states such as India.[28] Six hundred thousand Iraqi families subsisted on the government dole.[29] A team of experts funded by UNICEF (United Nations Children's Fund) and other multinational agencies determined, "Four times as many Iraqi children are dying today as before the Gulf crisis, 900,000 are malnourished and over 100,000 at immediate risk of starvation."[30] Electricity outages spoiled medicines, disrupted water purification and distribution, and terminated sewage treatment. In the fall of 1991, 60 percent of Iraqi households were without running water. Two-thirds of the available water sources were contaminated, causing epidemics of gastroenteritis, typhoid, and cholera. The death rate for children under five, 27.8 per thousand before the crisis, soared to 104.4 per thousand.[31]

Jordan

Iraq may be the Arab state most afflicted by the economic collapse of the 1980s and the damages of the Gulf War, but its problems are by no means unique. The economic dislocations triggered by the Gulf War extend from Morocco to Oman. For example, although Amman suffered no physical injury, the Gulf War dealt a devastating blow to the Jordanian economy. It ended both the cash grants Amman had received from Iraq and Kuwait ($185 million annually) and concessionary supplies of Iraqi oil which had covered 80 percent of Jordanian consumption. The UN embargo halted transit trade with Baghdad, which had supplied 6 percent of Jordan's GDP and employed 4 percent of its workforce, and idled the Aqaba port.[32] The Jordanian finance minister gave the International Monetary Fund (IMF) the most detailed accounting of economic losses prepared by any Arab state: he estimated that in the first year following the Iraqi invasion, the costs of the Gulf War to noncombatant Jordan would total $2,144 million—the equivalent of 63 percent of GNP.[33]

The lion's share of these losses could be traced to the Gulf War's disruption of the system of labor exchange. During the 1970s and 1980s, millions of Arabs from oil-poor countries like Jordan worked in the rich Gulf states. The money they sent home did more to redistribute petrodollars from the Gulf than intergovernmental aid and typically formed the largest source of hard currency for the poorer Arab states. But the Gulf War displaced five to six million people and effectively terminated this labor exchange.[34] Some workers fled to avoid the combat zone, but most were expelled by the Gulf states. For example, in September 1990

Saudi Arabia ordered Yemeni guestworkers and their families—at least 500,000 people—to leave the country. The Saudis claimed the action to be a sanction against the government of Yemen, which appeared to be sympathetic to Iraq. For similar reasons, the Saudis closed their border to trade with Jordan, depriving Amman of critical markets for agricultural exports.[35]

Kuwait dealt the mortal blow to Jordan's participation in the system of Arab labor exchange. Before the Iraqi invasion, two-thirds of Kuwait's population had been "resident alien" guestworkers and their families. After the invasion, the Kuwaitis started to view these workers as a disloyal fifth column, particularly the large community of resident Palestinians and Jordanians whose leaders had seemed to sympathize with Saddam Hussein. When Operation Desert Storm ended, the Kuwaitis systematically began to terrorize and expel these workers, often replacing them with smaller numbers of politically tractable Asians. In this way 300,000 Jordanian citizens were stripped of their jobs and forced to return to Amman by late 1991.[36]

The returnees increased the population of Jordan by 10 percent and raised the unemployment rate from 17 percent in 1990 to 25–30 percent by late 1991. Their arrival also meant an immediate loss of $320 million worth of hard currency remittances and a $220 million increase in imports to cover provisions for the returnees. The incidence of poverty in rural Jordan and the poorer neighborhoods of Amman soared as returnee families tried—and failed—to rejoin the local economy. This labor crisis, combined with the loss of trade, caused a 17 percent drop in Jordan's gross national product in 1990.[37]

As bad as things were in 1991, experts predicted that conditions in Jordan would worsen over the next several years. Some of the returnees arrived with savings or valuables, but these assets were consumed in the first year after their flight. Jordan's economic infrastructure groaned under the weight of the returnees, forcing the government to contemplate a massive program of investment—larger than it could afford—to prevent collapse. The government estimated that building housing, schools, sewer lines, electrical grids, and other facilities to meet the basic needs of the returnees by 1995 would cost at least $3.7 billion.[38] The damage to Jordan, as to Iraq, would reverberate throughout the economy for years to come.

The collapse of the system of labor exchange after the Gulf War was a watershed in the economic history of the Arab states. It seriously injured not only the economies of Jordan and the Yemen, but those of Egypt, the Sudan, and the West Bank. Combined with the interruption of trade and the diminution of inter-Arab aid flows, its effects were catastrophic.[39]

Calculating the cost of all these damages is a herculean task. Even the crudest estimates, however, elucidate the magnitude of the calamity. Edmund O'Sullivan in the *Middle East Economic Digest* estimates that Iraq alone is liable for damages that could reach $177 billion (table 2-1), a sum equal to the value of the combined exports of the Middle East and Africa for an entire year.[40] The International Monetary Fund, employing conservative figures, estimates that in 1991 the Gulf crisis led to a 4 percent drop in GDP for the Middle East as a whole, a 2.5 percent rise in the rate of inflation, and—despite a temporary rise in the price of oil—a decline in the region's current account from a $10 billion surplus to a $43 billion deficit.[41] Some Arab analysts claim that the total bill for physical damages, military costs, and economic dislocations arising from the Gulf War may reach $1,500 billion.[42] More moderate estimates hover around $500–$600 billion.[43]

Precision in calculating the costs of the Gulf War is unnecessary, however. Even if the lower-end estimates prove correct, it is clear that the Gulf War was an economic calamity for the Arab states. The resources of even the richest Arab states were sorely taxed by the crisis.

Saudi Arabia

Consider Saudi Arabia, which, like Jordan, suffered almost no physical damage during the Gulf War.[44] During the first month after Iraq invaded Kuwait, the Gulf was swept by a panic that caused economic dislocations. Many Saudi citizens prepared to flee abroad and began converting their savings accounts into dollars, which triggered a run on many banks. The Saudi stock market crashed, and 11 percent of all bank deposits were withdrawn. The government had to pump billions into the financial system to keep it from collapsing.[45] The Saudis also had to cope with an influx of refugees. Riyadh had to pay the airfare of thousands of Asian guestworkers who fled from Kuwait to the Kingdom, as well as provide shelter for 200,000 Kuwaiti nationals until their own government could set up a relief apparatus. Thousands of Saudi citizens were relocated from the combat zone in the Eastern Province,

Table 2-1. Cost of Iraq's Invasion and Occupation of Kuwait
Billions of dollars

Item	Amount
Cost of Operation Desert Storm	70
Loss of output and damage in Iraq	50
Physical damage to Kuwait	25
Loss of income to Kuwait	15
Loss of output in Arab countries	12
Loss of income in other countries	5
Total	177

Source: "Making Iraq Pay for Its War," *Middle East Economic Digest*, May 31, 1991, p. 4.

and an emergency civil defense system was created. The cost of these emergency measures totaled $8 billion.[46]

Moreover, the Saudis took the lead in providing financial incentives for countries that volunteered to serve in the coalition against Iraq. They paid the United States $16.8 billion and the United Kingdom $1 billion for their military services.[47] They offered at least $6 billion of assistance to other members of the coalition, such as Egypt, Syria, and Morocco, and even pledged funds to passive supporters of the coalition, such as Turkey ($1.2 billion) and the Soviet Union ($1.5 billion).[48]

The Saudis bore other costs as well. To help prepare the Kingdom's defenses, they spent at least $13 billion on new arms purchases through the end of 1990. In 1991, still reeling from the recent threat to their border, they concluded a host of new weapons contracts, including a $10 billion deal with the United States for three hundred M-1–A2 Abrams and M-60 tanks, four hundred armored personnel carriers, twenty-four F-15 fighter-bombers, twelve Apache helicopters, seven refueling planes, six Patriot antiballistic missile batteries, and six multiple-launch rocket systems.[49]

Another important way the Saudis contributed to the success of Operation Desert Storm was by ensuring against a shortfall in the global supply of oil. The UN embargo against Baghdad had cut off exports from Iraq and Kuwait totaling 4.35 million barrels per day (bpd). The Saudis made up the shortfall by increasing their own production from around 5 million bpd in August to 8 million bpd by December 1990. This expansion forced Riyadh to invest $4.7 billion in refurbishing or expanding pumping facilities and pipelines.[50]

Of course, expanded oil production, combined with a temporary rise in oil prices, augmented Saudi Arabia's cash flow. Saudi Arabia's petroleum exports were expected to produce windfall profits of $15 billion in 1990 and a similar amount in 1991.[51] Had there been no Gulf crisis, Riyadh might have shown a budget surplus for the first time in nearly a decade; the 1990 budget projected a $6.7 billion deficit. But the Gulf War loaded the Saudis with another $60–$80 billion of extraordinary expenses.[52] As Senator Everett M. Dirksen would have said, "A billion here, a billion there, and pretty soon you're talking about real money."

This was real money, even by Saudi standards. Saudi Arabia recorded current account deficits—which it paid by drawing down cash reserves—every year after 1983 (table 2-2).[53] Its 1991 current account deficit was expected to be the worst yet. The fiscal deficit was expected to be so large that the government did not even publish a budget; instead, line ministries were instructed to keep expenses within the budget posted for 1990.[54]

The Saudis could pay part of their Gulf War obligations from cash reserves, but these were no longer large enough to cover the full costs. The Saudi government claimed to have around $70 billion in assets in 1990, but many analysts suspected these figures included the value of uncollectible loans to Iraq, Egypt, and Morocco.[55] So Riyadh resorted to two other strategies to meet its commitments. First, it delayed payment as long as possible. Despite a pledge that the Kingdom would meet its obligations to the United States by the end of the U.S. fiscal year, by September 1991 the Saudis still owed the Americans $3.6 billion.[56] Second, the Saudi government began, for the first time, to borrow heavily on international markets. In May 1991 J. P. Morgan arranged a $4.5 billion loan for the Saudi government, which borrowed $2.5 billion more from domestic banks. In October the Saudi-state oil firm, Saudi Aramco, indicated it would borrow $1.5 billion internationally, and Riyadh announced that any future expansion of Saudi industries and firms would be financed primarily by borrowing rather than spending oil income. The Saudis planned to borrow particularly heavily from domestic banks, which had $20 billion in assets.[57]

These measures made it unlikely that Saudi Arabia would face bankruptcy—the Gulf crisis confronted Riyadh with "serious but short-term difficulties."[58] The rest of the Gulf states would also have to manage their finances carefully for the next two to five years by borrowing and postponing expenditures, after which conditions would ease. Even Kuwait, which had suffered more from the war than any Gulf state, was expected to weather the crisis. The Kuwaitis planned to meet their

Table 2-2. Indicators of Fiscal Pressure, by Country, 1980 and 1990

Country	Budget deficit as percent of government revenue		Percent change in government expenditures, 1980–90	Percent change in oil revenues, 1980–90	Percent change in government financial reserves, 1980–90
	1980	1990			
Algeria	0	3	305	38	-87
Bahrain	-15[a]	7	40	-8	-15
Egypt	14	27	349	5	68
Jordan	24	10	86	. . .	-51
Kuwait	-66[a]	68	53	-45	-67
Oman	-1[a]	22	113	36	89
Qatar	-42[a]	50	7	-37	21
Saudi Arabia	0	21	10	-62	-67
Tunisia	9	0	237	0	-12
United Arab Emirates	-13[a]	4	2	-20	49

Sources: International Monetary Fund (IMF), *International Financial Statistics Yearbook, 1991* (Washington, 1991); IMF, *International Financial Statistics, July 1992*, vol. 45, no. 7 (Washington, 1992); *The World in Figures* (London: The Economist Newspaper Limited, 1981); "Algeria: Hydrocarbons Income Set to Outstrip Earlier Forecasts," *Middle East Economic Digest* (MEED), September 14, 1990, p. 12; "Bahrain: Budget Deficit Likely to Grow," *MEED*, April 26, 1991, pp. 19–20; "Egypt: Tax Burden to Increase," *MEED*, June 7, 1991, p. 25; "Kuwait: Budget Set for Record Deficit," *MEED*, January 17, 1992, p. 15; "Oman: Budget Predicts Modest Spending Rise," *MEED*, January 11, 1991, pp. 17–18; "Oman: Oil Revenues Slash Budget Deficit," *MEED*, September 27, 1991, p. 25; Angus Hindley, "MEED Special Report: Qatar," *MEED*, October 4, 1991, p. 11; David Pike, "Riyadh Clears Its Crisis Debt," *MEED*, January 17, 1992, pp. 4–5; "Tunisia: Investment Set to Outstrip Predictions," *MEED*, August 10, 1990, p. 22; "UAE: Federal Budget Posts Dh 6 Billion Deficit," *MEED*, May 24, 1991, p. 31; and Angus Hindley, "MEED Special Report: UAE," *MEED*, November 29, 1991, p. 11.

. . . Insignificant value.

a. Fiscal surplus.

obligations by liquidating $22 billion of their foreign assets and borrowing another $35 billion overseas.[59]

The Arab states outside the Gulf, lacking the benefits of huge oil reserves and small populations, would take longer to recover. Only three (Egypt, Syria, and Morocco) had joined the coalition against Iraq and collected foreign assistance or debt relief as a reward; the rest could not expect much aid from their rich Gulf neighbors for the foreseeable future.[60] Even those that had joined the coalition were disappointed by niggardly subventions: Egypt virtually suspended relations with Kuwait when it discovered that there were no plans to promote the participation of Egyptian firms in the reconstruction of Kuwait, that Kuwaiti aid to Cairo would be in the form of interest-bearing loans rather than grants, and that Kuwait had cut off subventions for Egyptian troops in the Gulf.[61] Most of the poorer Arab states would be heavily tasked for the coming decade, coping with the loss of workers' remittances and reassimilating the laborers and professionals who had been forced to leave the Gulf.

The bottom line is that the Arab world, capital rich in 1980, today is capital poor. The global oil market, the major source of the region's wealth, remains relatively soft.[62] The Gulf War liquidated much of the cash reserves the Gulf states had built up during the boom years of the 1970s. What funds remain are being stretched to cover a host of competing expenditures. To remain creditworthy, the Arab states have to devote hefty funds to debt service. The rapid growth of population continues to generate pressure for expanded food imports and job creation. And for the next three to ten years, the budgets of many Arab states will be burdened by the cost of rebuilding the physical and economic damage wrought by the Gulf War.

Inevitably, the Arab world's reduced cash flow will mean fewer funds for arms purchases. Already in the late 1980s, as Arabs drifted toward economic crisis, there was a clear trend toward "de facto disarmament." Between 1987 and 1988 the combined military expenditures of Egypt, Jordan, Syria, and Israel fell from $9.8 billion to $9 billion, a decrease of 8.2 percent.[63] As Middle Eastern markets shrank, world arms sales declined by 24 percent, to $29.3 billion in 1989, their lowest level since 1983.[64] The economic damage inflicted by the Gulf War could, *ceteris paribus*, accelerate this trend.

However, exactly what part of revenue is allocated for military purposes is as much a political as an economic question. "Economic development is not a sort of ventriloquist with the rest of history as its dummy."[65] As budgets tighten, political leaders do not lay their axe equally on all categories of expenditure. If they so chose, they could insulate military expenditures from the general decline in spending by making deeper cuts in other areas. In the Middle East today, as it turns out, proponents of military spending are poorly positioned to insulate their budgets.

CHAPTER 3

The Politics of Arab Demilitarization

THE ECONOMIC PROBLEMS of the 1980s crested just as an unprecedented debate about the role of the military was developing in the Arab world. The prestige of the officer corps and the military establishment was at an all-time low. Ordinary citizens, not just governments, were beginning to think that the regional arms race was too expensive.

Signs of the debate were evident in Algerian parliamentary elections. In December 1991, in what was perhaps the freest ballot in Arab history, the Front Islamique du Salut (FIS) won 188 seats in the 430-member parliament. It was favored to win another 150 seats in the second round of balloting slated for January 1992, which would have given it the two-thirds majority necessary to rewrite the constitution and turn Algeria into an Islamic state.[1] Most of the elements of the FIS platform that swept it to victory were basically the same as those that have propelled the growth of Islamist movements across the Arab world. The FIS portrayed itself as the party of morality challenging a regime of corruption. It promised to restore economic growth by restricting government intervention and creating wider opportunities for private businessmen, and to defend the family or clan against the intrusions of the modern state by promoting the seclusion of women.[2] But one element of the campaign platform stood out: the FIS vowed to slash the defense budget to make more money available for social expenditures.[3]

The FIS promise to cut the defense budget was not decisive in its election victory; it probably was not even the leading cause of the military coup that denied the FIS access to office. But it was a symbol of an important change in Arab attitudes toward the military. The conviction that military spending was too high and social spending too low was widespread in all Arab states. Only the absence of democracy prevented that belief from being a centerpiece of the political agenda.

Table 3-1. **Regional Comparison of Military and Social Expenditures, 1986**

Region	Public education expenditure as percent of military budget	Public health expenditure as percent of military budget	Armed forces as percent of teachers
Arab states	46.0	14.3	183
Sub-Saharan Africa	115.2	27.3	90
South Asia	47.2	13.9	47
Asia	57.7	n.a.	66
Latin America	220.0	133.3	42
Industrial countries	111.1	153.7	105

Source: UN Development Programme, *Human Development Report, 1991* (Oxford University Press, 1991), tables 17, 19, 24, 38, and 40.
n.a. Not available.

In the decade after 1973, the Arab states exported roughly a trillion dollars' worth of petroleum products. During the same years, Arab regimes spent $300 billion to expand their militaries and $70 billion to import weapons. Even in these boom years, devoting a third of all revenues to the military meant crowding out investment in economic and social development. When oil revenues fell in the 1980s, military spending declined, but social investment fell even more rapidly. In the mid-1980s, the Iraqi government spent over seven times as much on its military as it did on health and education. In Syria the ratio was more than four to one.[4] Lopsided spending for the military characterized the entire region. (See table 3-1.)

Many Arabs blamed the disappointing levels of economic growth and social progress on the high level of military expenditures. Development in the Arab world in the 1970s and 1980s was unimpressive even by third world standards. Table 3-2 compares human development in various Arab and developing countries according to the human development index devised by the UN Development Program.[5] Despite petroleum wealth, no Arab state has attained the level of human development achieved by Costa Rica—and the majority of Arabs live in countries where the level of human development is lower than in Indonesia. Economic development was equally disappointing. Despite major industrialization drives, the combined manufacturing value added of all Arab states in 1989 was less than that produced in South Korea.[6] Between 1986 and 1989, the GNP per capita in Algeria, Egypt, Libya, Saudi Arabia, Syria, and South Yemen actually declined.[7]

Table 3-2. Human Development in Selected Arab and Developing Countries, 1992

Country	1990 population (millions)	1992 UN human development index	1990 life expectancy at birth (years)	1990 mortality rate for children under 5 (per 1,000 births)	1988 daily calorie supply (percent of requirements)	1990 adult literacy rate (percent)	1989 real GDP per capita (PPP$)[a]
Costa Rica	3.0	0.842	74.9	22	123	93	4,413
Kuwait	2.0	0.815	73.4	19	n.a.	73	15,984
Malaysia	17.9	0.789	70.1	29	119	78	5,649
United Arab Emirates	1.6	0.740	70.5	30	n.a.	55	23,798
Jamaica	2.5	0.722	73.1	20	115	98	2,787
Saudi Arabia	14.1	0.687	64.5	91	118	62	10,330
South Africa	35.3	0.674	61.7	88	125	70	4,958
Syria	12.5	0.665	66.1	59	127	65	4,348
Peru	21.6	0.600	63.0	116	94	85	2,731
Jordan	4.0	0.586	66.9	52	118	80	2,415
Iran	54.6	0.547	66.2	59	129	54	3,120
Algeria	25.0	0.533	65.1	98	112	57	3,088
Indonesia	184.3	0.491	61.5	97	120	77	2,034
Morocco	25.1	0.429	62.0	112	114	50	2,298
Zimbabwe	9.7	0.397	59.6	87	93	67	1,469
Egypt	52.4	0.385	60.3	85	127	48	1,934
India	853.1	0.297	59.1	142	94	48	910
Yemen	11.7	0.232	51.5	n.a.	95	39	1,560
Nepal	19.1	0.168	52.2	189	94	26	896
Mauritania	2.0	0.141	47.0	214	74	30	582
Arab total or weighted average	212.3	0.454	62.1	101	116	58	3,593

Source: UN Development Programme, *Human Development Report, 1992* (Oxford University Press, 1992). pp. 127–29, 134, 135, 170, 171, and 179.

n.a. Not available.

a. PPP$ is purchasing power parity dollars. Government currency controls and other factors make GDP per capita statistics converted at official exchange rates a poor indicator of real income levels. To correct for these distortions, the UN International Comparison Project has devised an international unit of account, the PPP$, which more accurately reflects real spending power.

It may have been unfair for Arabs to blame military expenditures or even conspicuous consumption in the Gulf states for all of their disappointment about development. The taproot of Arab economic failures instead may have been misguided governmental policies that failed to make effective use of available revenues.[8] But the stranglehold of Arab militaries on state budgets certainly obstructed development, as many were quick to point out. Already in the 1970s most Egyptians blamed their economic disappointments on the high cost of waging war in the Yemen. In the 1980s Syria and Iraq officially blamed slow economic growth on the cost of confronting Israel and Iran. Jordanians spoke eloquently about the "peace dividend" they hoped to obtain by settling their dispute with Israel: not only would peace permit military expenditures to be diverted to civilian purposes, it would create an atmosphere of security in which investments and foreign economic assistance might grow.[9]

Some academics argue against this popular perception, suggesting that military spending acts as seed money for the development of national industries, promotes technology transfers and the acquisition of new skills, and generally stimulates the economy.[10] Military industries certainly played an important role in the development of Japan and the newly industrialized countries of East Asia, and today may contribute to growth in Israel, Turkey, and Iran.[11] Fewer and fewer Arabs, however, find these examples compelling. Despite large areawide investment, the only Arab state in which military industrialization has made considerable progress is Egypt.[12] Even Cairo has been unable to find export markets for its arms (except in Iraq, which, despite its own much-advertised, multibillion-dollar military industrialization program, still relies heavily on weapons imports).[13] The only military-industrial complex that has developed in the Arab world is a purely mercantile one that links officials in defense ministries with civilian entrepreneurs who skim off a commission from arms import contracts.[14]

The perceived failure of military expenditures to contribute to development has been bad news for Arab governments, half of which are military regimes.[15] During the 1950s and 1960s, the heyday of the coup d'état in Arab politics, officers argued that the suspension of democratic liberties was a price that had to be paid for ensuring economic development and social equity.[16] They portrayed themselves as heirs of Kemal Ataturk, as instruments of modernization, and claimed that large military budgets provided wide public benefits. By the late 1980s, most

Arabs had grown tired of this "authoritarian bargain," feeling that they had traded away liberty without securing development.

Evolving Attitudes in the Officer Corps

Development failures were no less worrisome to officers than to civilians. Obviously, discontent over military expenditures threatened their mandate to rule. But more than that, many of them had been sincere disciples of Kemal Ataturk, and they were genuinely disappointed that the military had not been more successful in modernizing society. Most of all, they understood that the failure of economic development exacerbated Arab security problems and sapped the potency of the military itself.

Arab officers are far more sensitive than their counterparts in industrialized societies to the ways in which economic actions might undermine national security.[17] For example, many Arab states import more than 50 percent of their food needs (half of the world's ten most food-dependent countries are Arab), leaving them vulnerable to embargoes. In 1963 the United States suspended wheat shipments to Egypt to protest Cairo's military intervention in Yemen, and in 1973 Henry Kissinger raised the prospect of a food embargo in retaliation for the Arab oil embargo. The Saudi government responded with massive agricultural subsidies that have made the country a wheat exporter, and the Egyptian military developed an agricultural division that ensures its food self-sufficiency.[18] Arab officers have also taken measures designed to reduce their vulnerability to embargoes or controls on access to credit and strategic technologies. In an effort to make its operations self-financing, Syrian military intelligence learned to tap profits from Lebanon's drug trade. To evade foreign restrictions on the export of weapons-manufacturing machinery, Iraq's Ministry of Industry and Military Industrialization covertly acquired control over an international network of high-technology firms.[19] Over the long run, however, only domestic economic development can indemnify the Arab states from these foreign pressures.

There is a second, broader way in which Arab officers see economic development as central to their mission: the level of literacy, technical skills, and industrial capacity that prevails in a society directly affects the combat effectiveness of its military. In his analysis of Israel's crushing defeat of the combined armies of Egypt, Syria, and Jordan in 1967, *Self-Criticism after the Disaster*, Sadiq al-'Azm argued that the foremost reason for the dismal Arab performance in the war was rooted in the weaknesses of Arab society, not just in bad decisions by officers and politicians. Arab armies in 1967 consisted mostly of illiterate peasants, who were hostile to the distant elites that had sent them into battle, and who wielded foreign weapons they could neither use nor repair effectively. To prevail against Israel, al-'Azm said, the Arabs would have to learn the same lesson that Japan taught Russia in the war of 1905: only the modernization of society at large can produce the levels of technological competence and political commitment necessary for military victory.[20] Although only a minority of Arab officers embraced al-'Azm's proffered strategy of modernization—socialist revolution— many endorsed his wider argument.

By 1991 most Arab officers worried that disappointing socioeconomic development was eroding their authority and inhibiting their battlefield performance. They and their civilian compatriots saw plenty of evidence that Arab armies were still unable to effectively perform their assigned mission: to wage war.

Since 1967, no Arab army has been able to claim a clear battlefield victory. The 1973 attack by Syria and Egypt against Israel resulted in military defeat, even though it produced political benefits. Saddam Hussein boasted that he had won a great victory over Iran in 1988, but Tehran's decision to end the Iran-Iraq war resulted as much from damage inflicted by the U.S. Navy and international economic pressures as by the Iraqi military. In any case, Saddam's claims could disguise neither the strategic ineptitude of his 1980 decision to invade Iran nor the failure of the Iraqi army to prevail against its more poorly equipped opponents. The 1991 Gulf War may have been the most humiliating of all: even though it resulted in "the liberation of Kuwait," it showed the Arab forces involved to be third rate by international standards.

In 1991 the American, British, and French troops, who did most of the fighting for the allies, totally demolished the Iraqi military machine— the largest, best-equipped, and most expensive in the Arab world. On the first day of the war, allied air forces established air superiority and proceeded to bomb Baghdad with impunity. Allied ground forces outgunned and outmaneuvered their Iraqi counterparts, who surrendered en masse. Sustaining only minimal casualties themselves, the coalition took 65,000 Iraqi prisoners and killed 50,000–150,000. Even allowing that allied troops outnumbered the Iraqis two-to-one in the Kuwaiti theater of operations, it was a stunning victory.[21]

The troops Arab states had contributed to the alliance could claim little credit for the triumph.[22] Syria and Egypt supplied the best-trained Arab troops, but they generally avoided combat and their commanders privately admitted they were totally outclassed by the Western allies. According to some sources, all eighteen Egyptian troops who died in Operation Desert Storm were killed in accidents.[23] The armies of the Gulf states were even less impressive. Saudi ground forces proved poorly trained and weakly motivated; one Western observer described them as "a garrison army," highly dependent on "Filipino bottle washers and Pakistani mechanics."[24] Kuwaiti troops fought bravely, but their military contribution was hamstrung by their own government, which refused to arm them adequately for fear that officers—many of them critical of the regime—or troops—most of whom were not Kuwaiti citizens— might demand political influence after the war.

During three days of ground fighting, officers across the Arab world saw the prestige of their military machines evaporate. Even among Saddam's enemies, many were disappointed that the Iraqi army had not put up a more credible fight. In seventy-two hours, the armies that the Arabs had spent a generation building were proved obsolescent—adequate for riot control, perhaps, but not for modern warfare.[25]

In the aftermath of the Gulf War, stunned Arabs pondered how little security their petrodollar billions had purchased. In the Gulf states, which still had credit and some access to Western arsenals, officers could still dream of acquiring the new weapons that had devastated Iraq: global-positioning navigation aids and advanced battlefield intelligence systems, "standoff" missiles and smart bombs.[26] But most Arab states had neither the money nor the political influence necessary to obtain such high-technology imports, which was disconcerting especially for those Arab countries bordering Israel, the one state in the region with the capacity to manufacture and deploy such advanced conventional weapons.[27]

The Arab officer corps, economically constricted and militarily humiliated, saw its prestige reach its nadir in 1991. Latin American officers faced with similar conditions in the early 1980s (particularly the Argentine military after the Falkland Islands defeat) admitted their failure and withdrew from politics.[28] Some Arabs quietly hoped that their own officers would do likewise, creating an opportunity for the revival of democratization in the region.[29] Arab officers had other ideas.

In general, Arab officers resist surrendering power because they represent an exclusive and socially distinct elite, not just an occupational category. In Algeria and Egypt most senior officers come from the generation of old-fashioned Arab nationalists who are appalled by the Islamist currents so popular among civilians. In Sudan the leading officers are Islamists, unwilling to share power with the many less-stringent or non-Muslim groups in society. In Syria the upper echelons of the officer corps are dominated by Alawis, and in Iraq the most senior military commanders are Takritis—both groups are geographically localized religious minorities. In Saudi Arabia, of course, the most influential officers are all members of the Saud family.[30]

The distinctive identity of military elites in the Arab world has several politically significant effects. For one, the relatively closed character of the officer corps breeds resentment among the general population. Officers enjoy special economic privileges, such as access to subsidized housing, cars, special clubs, and stores, as well as political influence. For their part, officers are loath to relinquish their political power not only because these economic privileges might end, but because they fear the kin group or minority to which they belong might be victimized if their military protection is withdrawn. The 1979–82 civil war in Syria, the 1991 civil war in Iraq, and the 1992 coup in Algeria testify to how forcefully and effectively the officer elite will act to defend its power.[31]

Given that Arab officers will not voluntarily relinquish power, declining public support for military expenditures may seem a politically insignificant trend. Unless Arabs are willing to stage revolutions and drive their governments from power, what is to prevent current policies and policymakers from persisting? Recent developments in Syria provide an answer to this question.

Budget Battles in Syria

During the 1980s the Syrian economy suffered from the same general problems that plagued most Arab states: mismanaged state intervention had stifled production, and the cost of massive food and arms imports had led to a heavy debt burden.[32] But by 1989 conditions in Syria had begun to improve as crude oil production doubled. Syria was not heavily dependent on trade with the Gulf states or on workers' remittances, so the Gulf War left its economy relatively unscathed. Indeed, as a reward for joining the coalition against Iraq, Damascus received $700 million in credits from the Europeans and the Japanese and over $2 billion in cash or pledges from Saudi Arabia and the Gulf states.[33]

Most observers assumed that all of Syria's windfall from the Gulf War would be spent on arms imports. As early as 1988, rumors were circulating that the Syrians were pressing the Soviets to supply a multi-billion-dollar arms package.[34] After the Gulf War, the rumors took more concrete form. U.S. sources suggested the Syrians were lobbying Moscow for three hundred T-72 and T-74 main battle tanks, more than fifty MIG-29 fighters, early warning radar systems, and an array of SAM-11, SAM-13, and SAM-16 antiaircraft missiles, for a total value of $2 billion.[35] Israeli reports were even more alarming, claiming that Damascus also sought low-altitude Sukhoi-24 bombers, advanced Sukhoi-27 fighters, surface-to-surface missiles, and a Soviet equivalent of the U.S. Patriot antitactical ballistic missile system.[36]

The Syrians appeared to have two other major arms purchases in the works. In March 1991, Israel announced that North Korea had supplied Syria with twenty-four launchers for Scud-C missiles, which could carry a heavier payload than the Scud-B missiles that Iraq had used against Israel and Saudi Arabia during the Gulf War.[37] Although these reports met with some skepticism—some experts thought that the North Koreans did not have the capacity to produce Scud-Cs—the Israelis took them seriously enough to plan an attack in October on a North Korean freighter they believed was transporting missiles for Damascus.[38] Details about the deal with Pyongyang were sketchy, but the purchase reportedly included at least sixty missiles costing over $1 million apiece.[39] In May, various reports claimed that Czechoslovakia, confronting rising unemployment as it tried to move away from a centrally planned economy, also had agreed to sell Syria three hundred mothballed T-72 tanks for the bargain-basement price of $200 million.[40]

By late 1992, however, the expected rearmament of Syria had not materialized.[41] Moscow signed no new arms agreement. In 1992 the Czechs announced that they would complete a standing contract for the delivery of T-72 tanks to Damascus but would not make any future sales.[42] The North Korean ship suspected of carrying missiles returned to port without docking in Syria, and in February 1992 a second freighter

Table 3-3. Foreign Debt of the Arab States, 1990

Country	Total debt stocks (millions of U.S. dollars)	Total debt service (millions of U.S. dollars)	Total debt stocks as percent of gross national product	Total debt service as percent of exports of goods and services	Percent growth of total debt stocks since 1980
Algeria	26,806	8,256	52.9	59.4	38.3
Egypt	39,885	3,405	126.5	25.7	90.1
Jordan	7,678	709	225.7	24.6	288.4
Lebanon	1,931	148	n.a.	n.a.	293.7
Mauritania	2,227	69	226.7	13.9	163.9
Morocco	23,524	1,948	97.1	23.4	142.3
Oman	2,484	769	n.a.	13.0	314.7
Sudan	15,383	49	163.2	5.7	197.9
Syria	16,446	1,467	118.1	26.9	363.4
Tunisia	7,534	1,519	62.4	25.8	113.6
Yemen	6,235	158	n.a.	8.2	270.2

Source: World Bank, *World Debt Tables, 1991–92*, vol. 2, *Country Tables* (Washington, 1991), pp. 2, 122, 202, 218, 254, 266, 294, 378, 386, 410, and 438.
n.a. Not available.

supposedly carrying Scuds for Damascus failed to reach the Mediterranean, although it did make port in Iran.[43]

No one doubted that the Syrian military had hoped to go on a shopping spree, but several factors crimped their planned binge. International pressures played an important role. Syrians had hoped since the late 1980s to purchase 150 M-9 surface-to-surface missiles from China; the Bush administration, however, had successfully lobbied China to halt the sale.[44] In April 1987 General Secretary Mikhail Gorbachev announced that he felt Syria's arms buildup was damaging the Syrian economy and threatening to destabilize the region; thereafter the Soviets critically reviewed and restricted Syrian arms requests.[45] Following the breakup of the Soviet Union, the members of the Commonwealth of Independent States, particularly Russia, seemed inclined to sustain Gorbachev's policy.[46]

Perhaps if the Syrians had been able to plunk large wads of cash on the table, their negotiations with the Russians might have succeeded. But despite the improvement in Syria's economic fortunes, Damascus did not give its negotiators the authority to do just that. In addition to international pressures, domestic pressures in Syria prevented the government from dedicating $2 billion to arms imports.[47]

The Syrian government in fact controlled less cash than its improving national accounts might have suggested. Some of the subventions from the Gulf states came as pledges or with strings attached, but most of the military's cash shortfall arose because cabinet ministers and bureaucrats had successfully earmarked a lot of government funds for nonmilitary purposes.

During the economic crisis of the late 1980s, debt service problems had threatened to overwhelm Syria's ability to do international business, civilian or military (see table 3-3). The Soviets and the Czechs refused to conclude new arms deals until Syria made arrangements to settle its arrears; the Chinese and Koreans insisted upon payment in cash. Damascus fell $300 million behind in its payments to the World Bank and found it difficult to obtain credit for trade with the West. To deal with these problems, Syria's civilian technocrats were granted unprecedented authority.[48] To restore economic growth, these technocrats successfully lobbied for liberalization of foreign exchange controls, assorted incentives to lure back wealthy expatriates, and a new investment law guaranteeing wider latitude for private entrepreneurs.[49] They made sure that debt service had first claim on government funds.[50]

With their newfound authority, the technocrats also ensured that economic projects retained high priority even after the Gulf crisis had eased the government's cash crunch. They competed successfully with the officer corps for claims on government funds. They argued that investing the Gulf War windfall in the economy would ultimately generate more revenue, even for the military, than would spending it immediately on arms imports—in other words, they promised they could get more bang for the buck. For example, one minister appealed to the president for $200 million for the construction of a steel plant in Hama. He contended that he could use these funds as leverage to lure Gulf governments into loaning the remaining $300 million he needed to fund the plant.[51] The government gave him the money.

Civilian technocrats were encouraged by such examples. They learned that if they could get the government to fund part of a project, they might be able to find private or foreign capital to fund the rest. They learned that if they could get a project started, they would later be in a position to argue that the government should fund its completion. In the first nine months of 1991, Syrian ministries issued $2 billion in civilian tenders. No one believed that all of the projects would be funded, but they clearly proved that the technocrats were bidding for—and hoped to win a large share of—the cash contributions the government received from the Gulf.

In April 1992 some of these budget battles began to be waged in public. For the first time in decades, delegates in the Syrian people's assembly declined to rubberstamp the government's budget. Instead, they criticized the finance minister's proposed budget, arguing that it did not allocate enough to social expenditures. In particular, they wanted to see more funds allocated to help Syrians cope with rising inflation and growing unemployment.[52]

Civilian technocrats and politicians became bolder, partly because they understood that public opinion was on their side. In the late 1980s, no funds had been available for investment in Syria's economic infrastructure; enterprises and public buildings had fallen into shabbiness and disrepair. Inflation ran as high as 60 percent annually, but there had been no funds to raise the wages of public sector employees, who formed half of the nonagricultural workforce.[53] Most Syrians agreed that the economy deserved priority over the military in the state budget. Many Syrians began to argue publicly that the country's real battle was not with Iraq or even Israel; rather, they said, "Our war is against poverty."[54]

The government's foreign policy had inadvertently encouraged this shift in attitudes. For many years, fear of Israel had not only legitimated military expenditures but bound otherwise contentious Syrians to a common national purpose.[55] But Hafiz al-Asad's quest to attain strategic parity with Israel had failed to win Arab support and drained the economy.[56] In 1989 Asad himself had retreated from this policy by seeking rapprochement with Egypt. In July 1991 he went a step further by agreeing to join American-sponsored face-to-face peace talks with Israel. These moves left most Syrians convinced that their dispute with Israel would be resolved by negotiation rather than military action. Support for a national military buildup faded.

Moreover, during the two years before the Gulf War, Syrians found out just what the efforts to build up their military had cost them in the past. During the 1980s the Syrians had built up $12 billion in military debts to the Soviet Union. Syria did not have the hard currency to service this debt, so in 1989 Moscow agreed to take payment in Syrian pounds. As part of the deal, Damascus signed a commercial convention that permitted the Soviets to use their pounds to buy and export any goods from Syria except oil and phosphates (which could be used to generate hard currency).[57]

Accordingly, the Soviets went on a shopping spree. They began buying up a large share of Syrian fruit and vegetable crops. Syrian textile manufacturers and clothesmakers began gearing up to produce cheap copies of French fashions for the eastern European market. In 1989 Syria showed its first trade surplus in thirty years.[58] In 1991 the Soviet consul in Aleppo, who acted as his government's agent for many large purchases, bragged that he had made "more millionaires in the last two years than the Syrian government had in the preceding twenty."

Thanks to Soviet spending in a liberalized economic environment, some Syrians, particularly those in the private sector, suddenly became much wealthier. Others, particularly those working for fixed government salaries, faced a wave of inflation and felt much poorer.[59] Both groups, however, came to realize what a difference $12 billion worth of spending could make to their economy. And they came to appreciate just how much they had sacrificed in the past when these funds had been diverted to military purposes.

It is perhaps too early to say whether the combination of public pressure and technocratic maneuvering will lead to continued and significant reductions in Syrian military expenditures, but it seems likely that a large share of Syria's Gulf War windfall will be diverted from military to civilian purposes. At any rate, certainly the battle over the budget has delayed arms spending. The Syrian officer corps will likely go on buying weapons, too, but far fewer than they had wanted or their enemies had feared. With the right combination of international pressures, the final am unt devoted to the military might be reduced substantially.

From Demilitarization to Arms Control

The trends apparent in Syria, which is under less economic pressure than most Arab states, are evident elsewhere in the Middle East, often with even greater force. There is a growing disappointment with the military and a stronger demand for peace. There is an enhanced appreciation of how much money has been squandered on arms and a conviction that in the future economic development should take priority. In some states there is even evidence that the balance of power within regimes is slowly tipping away from the military in favor of civilian competitors.

It is likely that, for the next few years, there will be a strong trend toward demilitarization in the Middle East. Most countries will lack the hard currency necessary to continue the scale of arms imports they indulged in during the 1980s. Many will have to cap or even reduce their domestic military spending. All will search for cheaper means to provide national security.

CHAPTER 4

Arab Arms Control Initiatives

IN THEIR EFFORTS to shave military budgets, Middle Eastern states confront a frightening question. Can they maintain a credible national defense with the reduced funds at their disposal?

Three plausible ways to do so are being explored. First, some regimes hope to acquire alternative military technologies that provide more "bang for the buck." They hope that by buying more antitank missiles for a couple of thousand dollars apiece they will not have to buy as many tanks, which can cost more than a million dollars each. The rush by some states to import ballistic missiles needs to be understood in this light. Missiles can perform many of the same missions as advanced combat aircraft, but are much cheaper and more readily available on international markets. Developing countries "may not be able to afford or absorb stealth technology for now, but they can certainly seek advanced cluster munitions, fuel-air explosives, and sea-launched cruise missiles."[1]

Generally, however, the switch to less expensive technologies seems to involve a tangible loss in military power. Economical weapons systems are not as versatile as the more expensive alternative they substitute for: antitank missiles cannot perform the full array of missions that tanks can. Jet fighters are more accurate than ballistic missiles, and by flying repeated missions they can deliver explosives more cheaply than single-fire rockets.[2] Arab states have sought ballistic missiles not because they can fully substitute for advanced jet fighters, but because high prices and export restrictions have denied them access to the jets they would prefer.[3] Economical weapons do not make budget cutting painless.

A second approach seeks gains in military efficiency from a different type of economy: the elimination of waste. Some officers advocate demobilizing units of half-trained and halfhearted conscripts and focusing what funds remain on training and equipping a smaller force of military professionals. In this way, Middle Eastern armies would become smaller but fiercer, or "leaner but meaner."[4]

But this approach too has limitations. The economies involved seem to be either small or nonexistent: in the Middle East, the cost of training and outfitting one military professional may equal that of dragooning a half-dozen conscripts. To save much money, the size of the armed forces would have to be reduced drastically; the effects on the length of the border it could defend or the size of the territory it could hold would be drastic as well.[5]

Economization strategies can temper the effects of budget cuts, but they cannot completely offset them. The gains in efficiency they create are small relative to the size of the budget reductions Middle Eastern militaries face. Most Middle Eastern economies can no longer finance the current level of military capacities; they will have to accept a real reduction. Military budgets will have to be trimmed of more than fat—cuts in muscle must be made. Recognition of this hard fact has bred interest in a third approach to the problem: arms control.

Arms Control Proposals

In the industrial countries of the West—which can afford to build and maintain huge arsenals—arms control is commonly portrayed as an idealistic and altruistic program, motivated simply by the desire to live in peace. In economically troubled developing countries, the perception is quite different: arms control is often viewed as a way for the state to deny its adversaries weapons that it cannot afford itself. Arms control agreements allow a state to reduce its own arsenal and thereby cut its military budget, while similar reductions among its opponents ensure that overall security is unaffected. That arms control in the third world may be motivated by cold economic calculations does not make such programs any less viable than their counterparts in the West. In fact, economic motives may prove more reliable and durable than warm, fuzzy musings about peace. More important, economic considerations could induce arms control even in regions that lack the complex conditions necessary for conflict resolution and peacemaking.

Spurred by their economic crisis, Arab regimes have endorsed a number of arms control proposals since the end of the Gulf War. For example, Egypt and a dozen other states embraced President Bush's May 1991 arms control initiative. Egyptian President Hosni Mubarak saw the Bush plan as a variation of his own proposal submitted to the United Nations in 1990 to control the spread of weapons of mass destruction in the region. The Mubarak plan, in turn, built on a series of Egyptian efforts that Cairo had been pressing since 1974 to promote creation of a nuclear-free zone in the Middle East.[6]

Economic motives underpinned Egypt's strong interest in nuclear nonproliferation. As early as the 1960s Cairo had decided that any program to develop nuclear weapons would be too expensive to sustain.[7] The experience of the one Arab state that implemented an extensive nuclear development program, Iraq, testifies to the wisdom of the Egyptian decision.

Iraq launched its nuclear weapons program in 1974, when the oil boom seemed to free Baghdad of financial constraints. The initial plan was to acquire "civilian" nuclear reactors and use them to generate plutonium, which could be secretly diverted for use as fissile material in weapons. Iraq purchased two nuclear reactors from France for $3 billion.[8] It also spent $4–$8 billion to construct nuclear research facilities and to train Iraqi nuclear engineers and recruit nuclear scientists from other Arab states.[9] But the effort to build plutonium-based nuclear weapons succumbed in 1981 to successful Israeli sabotage, which culminated in an airstrike that demolished the Tammuz II reactor.[10]

Baghdad did not abandon its nuclear ambitions, however. Instead it launched a new program to enrich uranium to weapons grade. Uranium-enrichment facilities are less susceptible to exposure or sabotage than plutonium-generating reactors, but they are also more expensive to construct. Despite the cost, Baghdad launched two uranium-enrichment programs to hedge against the likelihood that difficulties in smuggling or operating the high-technology equipment might stall a single effort.[11] One program, which attempted to enrich uranium electromagnetically, operated from a facility at Tarmiyah that included a 100-megawatt power supply, several 25-ton cranes, a hermetically sealed air system, and its own purified water supply.[12] This program alone may have cost as much as $8 billion. A second, even more secret, program was launched in 1988 to try to enrich uranium using arrays of sophisticated centrifuges in plants at al-Furat and al-Sharqat. Enrichment centrifuges are notoriously difficult to manufacture, so even the optimistic Iraqis did not expect to have these plants fully operational before 1996.[13]

In addition to uranium-enrichment facilities, the Iraqi nuclear program called for a number of other factories. Baghdad invested $200 million in a world-class research and engineering facility, Sa'd-16, to supply machine tools for its nuclear and other weapons programs.[14] To acquire carbonrotors for its centrifuges, computer-operated lathes for Sa'd-16, and other material for its weapons programs, Iraq created an extensive network of semiclandestine overseas holding companies financed by $3 billion worth of unsecured letters of credit from the Atlanta branch of the Banca Nazionale del Lavoro.[15] Inside Iraq, Baghdad funded a phosphate mine at Akashat for uranium ore extraction, a yellowcake processing center at al-Qa'im, a uranium gas separation plant at al-Jesira, and a weaponization plant at al-Atheer that was charged with figuring out how to assemble enriched uranium, high explosives, and sophisticated electronics into a workable bomb.[16]

The total cost of Baghdad's nuclear program is difficult to estimate, but during the 1980s alone Iraq certainly spent at least $10 billion and probably as much as $20 billion in pursuit of a bomb.[17] Despite this commitment, in 1991 Iraq still did not have a workable design for a bomb and was still three to five years away from having enough enriched uranium to construct a viable nuclear device.[18] Operation Desert Storm demolished many of the Iraqi nuclear program's key facilities, and after the war special UN inspection teams supervised destruction of most of the surviving elements. Viewed as a "technology transfer" project, the Iraqi nuclear program may be the most expensive single failure in the history of the third world.

With the collapse of the Iraqi program, there is little prospect that any Arab state will build its own nuclear weapons in the next ten years.[19] Poorer Arab states, such as Egypt, Jordan, and Morocco, cannot afford to build a bomb. Richer Arab states, such as Saudi Arabia and Kuwait, have little incentive to do so: launching a nuclear weapons program could jeopardize their invaluable security ties to the United States.[20]

This leaves the Arabs in an uncomfortable position. Israel already has a nuclear arsenal of at least 200 weapons, including boosted fission bombs and neutron bombs, and it has the capability to manufacture hydrogen bombs.[21] Pakistan and Kazakhstan also already have nuclear armaments. The next Middle Eastern state to produce nuclear weapons is likely to be Iran, which possesses the technical resources necessary for their production.[22] Arab leaders see a clear trend toward a dichotomy in the Middle East, with one order made up of non-Arab states that do have the bomb, the other of Arab states that do not.[23]

This is why support for the creation of a nuclear weapons-free zone in the Middle East is nearly universal among Arab leaders.[24] Since they cannot afford to build such weapons themselves, they would be happy to forswear them if they could get their adversaries to do likewise. Iraq and Syria have offered to sweeten such a deal by extending it to other weapons of mass destruction: they are willing to dismantle their arsenals of chemical weapons if nuclear weapons can be banned from the region.[25] (Arab officers remain skeptical about the utility of chemical weapons against military targets, viewing them primarily as an instrument of political leverage which might be used to deter enemy attacks or as a bargaining chip in arms control talks. Arab officers are thus quite sincere when they argue that chemical weapons are "the poor man's atomic bomb.")[26] Egypt and other supporters of the Bush proposal to limit Middle Eastern production of nuclear weapons indicated they would go further: they would agree to stop producing nuclear weapons themselves and leave Israel's nuclear arsenal intact.[27] This proposal, which accepts the principal of asymmetrical arms control arrangements—allowing Israel to retain a temporary advantage over Arab neighbors—represents an important type of "new thinking" in the Middle East.

Certain Egyptian and Palestinian arms control experts argue that by forswearing production of their own nuclear weapons and leaving Israel with a nuclear monopoly, the Arabs could demonstrate a measure of realism about the technological balance in the region and at the same time gain concrete political advantages. Within Israel, the Labor party and the Left have been much more reluctant than the Likud party and the Right to contemplate any curb on Israel's nuclear capacities. This apparent paradox, in which "doves" favor retention of nuclear weapons while "hawks" show more flexibility, reflects a savvy political calculation. Labor is prepared to negotiate "land-for-peace" with the Arabs; the Likud is not. Labor leaders argue that, if Israel relinquishes control of some of the territories it captured in the 1967 war, it will need its nuclear monopoly to offset the resultant loss of "strategic depth."[28] Thus, some experts say, by accepting Israel's nuclear monopoly, the Arabs could strengthen the hand of Labor and lay the foundations for recovery of the territories lost in 1967.

The merits of tolerating Israel's nuclear monopoly have been hotly debated in the Arab world, particularly by Palestinians, who have the greatest stake in restoring Arab rule to the occupied territories.[29] The Palestinians have led the way in contemplating confidence-building measures that might prompt Israel to be more flexible in peace talks and more forthcoming about territorial concessions: Palestinian experts have proposed, among other measures, the creation of demilitarized zones and limited force zones, the stationing of multinational peacekeeping forces and electronic early-warning sensors, and various limitations on the configuration of Arab forces to ensure their *defensive* character.[30] In the view of these experts, Arab nuclear disarmament could be combined with an array of controls on conventional forces to counter the Israeli Right's strategic rationale for retaining the occupied territories.

Of course, Palestinians find it easier than other Arabs to consider radical arms control proposals. The Palestinians have no state and no standing army; even their guerrilla forces represent a much smaller commitment (measured in terms of combatants as a share of overall population) than the forces of any Arab government. They can contemplate limitations on force size and armaments that might someday be deployed in the West Bank and Gaza because a conventional Palestinian army does not now exist. It is much more difficult politically for an Arab state to embrace arms control arrangements that would reduce the numbers and weapons of an existing—and influential—military establishment.

Jordan's Arms-for-Debt Proposal

Yet, difficult or not, some Arab states have already begun to reduce their defense budgets and even the size of their forces. Jordan, in particular, has played a leading role in this effort.

Except for Iraq's and Kuwait's, no Arab economy suffered as much damage from the Gulf War as Jordan's. The war saddled Amman with hundreds of thousands of refugees, choked off the critical flow of hard currency from workers' remittances, closed the markets of its largest trading partners, and terminated most of its foreign aid. As a result, Jordan lacked the money necessary to sustain its military and had to make drastic budget cuts.[31] Amman canceled its billion-dollar contract to purchase Mirage jet fighters from France and suspended a similar contract for Tornado fighter-bombers.[32] Jordan even tried to sell some of the F-5 fighters and M-48 tanks already in its arsenal in a desperate attempt to generate cash.[33]

The Jordanian military began to shed manpower as well as hardware. King Hussein pressed a bill through parliament that abolished universal military conscription.[34] The number of men under arms declined from 130,000 at the beginning of 1991 to 107,000 by the end of the year, and was expected to drop to 95,000 by the fall of 1992.[35] A restructuring of forces accompanied the downsizing: one of Jordan's two mechanized divisions was downgraded to a light division.[36]

These unilateral arms reductions were obviously risky for Jordan. The measures saved money but eroded Amman's ability to resist political pressures from Israel, Syria, and Iraq, all of which had a history of intervening in Jordanian affairs. The Jordanians, naturally, were eager to encourage their neighbors to make similar cuts in order to restore the relative balance of forces among them.

In looking for a strategy for promoting arms control, Jordanian leaders were inspired by the Conference on Security and Cooperation in Europe (CSCE), which had played an important role in negotiating mutual force reductions between NATO and Warsaw Pact forces.[37] In 1990 Italy took the lead in attempts to extend the CSCE model to other regions, negotiating the formation of a parallel organization, the Conference on Security and Cooperation in the Mediterranean, which included several Arab states (Algeria, Libya, Mauritania, Morocco, and Tunisia).[38] The Jordanians proposed to build on the model by creating another body, the Conference on Security and Cooperation in the Middle East (CSCME), which would include the eastern Arab world.[39]

The Jordanians hoped that the CSCME would permit member states to negotiate common arrangements for dealing with a host of issues: labor migration, oil prices, water supplies, terrorist organizations, and so on. But Amman hoped the central focus of CSCME, like CSCE, would be arms control. To encourage that concentration, Jordan floated a bold proposal to link debt reduction and arms control. The Jordanians observed that in the past the two problems had been joined in a vicious circle: expensive debt service stifled Arab economies and bred poverty, poverty fueled violence, violence stimulated arms purchases, arms purchases required foreign borrowing, foreign borrowing aggravated the debt crisis, and on and on. To break the circle, the Jordanians suggested the following:

The successful implementation of arms control and arms reduction will release substantial funds that were previously wasted on armaments. Countries abiding by such a process will qualify for the systematic and measured reduction of existing debts (most of which were accumulated through arms purchases in the first place). A cursory look at most indebted nations in the Middle East reveals that most, if not all, would no longer need continuous subsidies if the existing debt overhead is removed (this includes Turkey, Israel and Iraq). The key issue, however, is not the write-off of debts in a vacuum. It should be part of an arms control and reduction package coupled with appropriate economic adjustment policies (stabilization and structural adjustments).[40]

The Jordanians found the allure of an arms-for-debt swap irresistible. Amman was saddled with more than $8 billion in foreign debts; it had suspended payment on bilateral debts in 1989, and had to raise more than $300 million a year just to service its public debt.[41] Consequently, Jordan wanted to reschedule its debts, but the IMF would agree to rescheduling only if Jordan adopted an economic adjustment program, including drastic cuts in subsidies on consumer staples and an increase in prices for electricity and other government services. The last IMF adjustment program that Jordan had embraced, in April 1989, had triggered five days of rioting that rocked the monarchy.[42] In contrast, an arms-for-debt swap would allow the burden of adjustment to be shared between the military and the civilian population. It would achieve debt reduction rather than just debt rescheduling. And it would transform the reduction of the military budget from a simple economic necessity into an act of political virtue.

Jordan was not the only Middle Eastern state, however, to which an arms-for-debt swap appealed. A majority of Arab states were heavily indebted (see table 3-3 in chapter 3). Many had tried to win approval for debt rescheduling by adopting IMF-style austerity programs. Such programs had triggered riots in Egypt, Tunisia, and Morocco and ignited virtual revolutions in Algeria and Sudan.[43] Any proposal that would allow them to reduce their heavy burden of debt service without running the gauntlet of popular protests against austerity measures was bound to receive close and sympathetic attention.

There was also reason to believe an arms-for-debt swap would be of interest to the Arab world's creditors. Various debt swaps, such as the debt-for-nature swap designed to promote sound ecological policies in Latin America, had been proposed before but none had been especially successful.[44] In the Middle East conditions were different. In Latin

America most foreign debt had been borrowed from private lenders, who were unenthusiastic about forgoing profits—much less forgiving their loans—in order to achieve some public good. In contrast, in the Arab world most overseas debt was owed to foreign governments, who might be more amenable to achieving a public goal like arms control.

Moreover, in Latin America advocates of debt swaps had to compete with an appealing alternative: many creditors thought that, with some improvement in management, Latin American economies could grow rapidly enough to properly service their debt.[45] Most Middle Eastern economies, in contrast, were in such poor shape that few believed their debts would ever be repaid. In fact, many Western governments were already contemplating forgiving some or all Middle Eastern debts: these loans were practically uncollectible, yet default could lead to a rupture with strategically important states in the region.[46] The United States had forgiven $7 billion in debts owed by Egypt in September 1990. France had canceled debts owed by the Yemen, and President François Mitterrand urged Western countries to devise a general program of debt forgiveness for the poorest states in Africa and the Arab world.[47] Hence an arms-for-debt swap would have the same effect on creditor nations that it would have on debtor states: it would transform an economic necessity into a political virtue.[48]

The IMF might even support this sort of program. For years the Fund's assessment of an economy's soundness had been based entirely on the government's economic policies: How large is the fiscal deficit? Is the currency overvalued? How much are private sector activities regulated? But a series of studies conducted in the late 1980s convinced the Fund's administration that it had to examine a country's military spending as well. These studies provided strong statistical evidence for the common-sense proposition that countries with high levels of military expenditures tend to save less, and hence their economies tend to grow more slowly.[49] More disturbing, they suggested that military expenditures were generally insulated from the burden of adjustment when the Fund arranged loans or debt rescheduling for a country.[50] These findings suggested the importance of viewing military spending as a development issue.

Michel Camdessus, managing director of the IMF, was persuaded that the Fund had to begin working toward reducing the military budgets of developing countries. Immediately after the Gulf War, he urged industrialized nations to ban export credits for weapons sales to the

Table 4-1. Hypothetical Arms-for-Debt Swap at a 1:2 Ratio, 1987
Millions of dollars unless otherwise specified

Country[a]	Military expenditures	Military expenditures as percent of GNP	Total external debt	Value of a 20 percent reduction in military expenditures	Value of debt forgiven	Percent of total debt retired
Algeria	1,486	2.9	26,944	297.2	594.4	2.2
Bahrain	160	5.6	. . .	32.0	64.0	. . .
Egypt	8,038	11.5	49,628	1,607.6	3,215.2	6.5
Israel	6,101	14.6	26,332	1,220.2	2,440.4	9.3
Jordan	590	13.9	5,279	118.0	236.0	4.5
Kuwait	1,330	5.2	. . .	266.0	532.0	. . .
Lebanon	n.a.	n.a.	496	n.a.	n.a.	n.a.
Libya	2,900	12.9	. . .	580.0	1,160.0	. . .
Mauritania	37	4.2	1,977	7.4	14.8	0.7
Morocco	1,156[b]	7.0	18,975	231.2	462.4	2.4
Oman	1,518	20.8	2,850	303.6	607.2	21.3
Qatar	n.a.	n.a.	. . .	n.a.	n.a.	. . .
Saudi Arabia	16,210[b]	19.4	. . .	3,242.0	6,484.0	. . .
Sudan	194[b]	2.7	10,562	38.8	77.6	0.7
Syria	1,472[b]	11.5	4,695	294.4	588.8	12.5
Tunisia	288[b]	3.2	6,476	57.6	115.2	1.8
U.A.E.	1,590	6.7	. . .	318.0	636.0	. . .
Yemen (N)	310	6.5	2,631	62.0	124.0	4.7
Yemen (S)	n.a.	n.a.	1,930	n.a.	n.a.	n.a.

Sources: U.S. Arms Control and Disarmament Agency, *World Military Expenditures and Arms Transfers, 1989* (1990), pp. 36–70; World Bank, *World Debt Tables, 1989–90. First Supplement* (Washington, 1990), pp. 38–245; and World Bank, *World Development Report, 1989* (Oxford University Press, 1989), *passim*.

n.a. Not available.

. . Insignificant value.

a. Figures are not available for Iran and Iraq.

b. Estimate.

Middle East.[51] In October 1991 he reached an agreement with his counterpart at the World Bank, Lewis Preston: both agencies would consider halting support for governments that spent too much on their militaries.[52] An arms-for-debt swap might prove to be an elegant tool with which the Fund could press its plan to rationalize the economies of the developing countries.

The Jordanian call for an arms-for-debt swap has not yet been endorsed by any other country or agency, partly because it is not yet a fully drawn proposal. It is only a sketch with no details penciled in. Those details could prove extremely important for both creditor and debtor states.

For example, the gearing ratio of the swap—the formula specifying how many dollars of debt will be forgiven in exchange for each dollar reduction in military expenditures—is critical. The ratio must be higher than 1:1 to act as an incentive to debtor nations. Indeed, an arms-for-debt swap will have greatest appeal if it offers debtor states an opportunity to cancel their obligations in a relatively short period; politicians are generally unenthusiastic about programs whose benefits materialize only after they leave office.

Conversely, creditor nations would not want the gearing ratio to be too high. A very high ratio would allow debtor states to cancel their debts quickly while making a relatively small cut in their arms programs; the ratio must be kept fairly low to ensure that military expenditure reductions are significant and sustained. Sustaining a cut in defense budgets over a prolonged period is particularly important. If such a reduction continues over several years, lower levels of defense spending might very well become the norm, because all the states in the region could feel more secure as growing numbers cut military expenditures or because civilian agencies institutionalize effective claims to a larger share of the budget.

Table 4-1 illustrates the practical implications of this problem. It shows how an arms-for-debt swap would work in one year if participating debtors made a big but not draconian cut of 20 percent in their military budgets, and the gearing ratio were 1:2 (that is, each dollar reduction in military expenditures would yield a two-dollar reduction of debt). Under these conditions, some of the more eager arms consumers in the region—including Egypt, Israel, Jordan, and Syria—would be able to retire their foreign debts in under twenty years. But some of the poorer states in the region would need more than a century to liquidate their debt. Sudan and Mauritania, for example, would have to eliminate their military budgets entirely to even come close to canceling their debts in twenty years. Happily, gearing ratios can be varied so that heavily in-debted states receive enough debt relief to encourage their participation in the program.

Any arms-for-debt initiative would be synergistic: as more and more states subscribed to the program, their neighbors would feel more secure about following suit. Some of the poorer Arab states, such as Yemen, may be so desperate for debt relief that they might follow the Jordanian example and unilaterally endorse an arms-for-debt swap. In fact, in 1992 fiscal pressures had forced Yemen to cut its military budget by 12 percent and to reduce the size of its armed forces by 12.5 percent.[53] A few others, such as Algeria, have so little to fear from their neighbors that they might seize upon the economic benefits of such a program without waiting for matching arms reductions by their neighbors.

Most Middle Eastern states, however, would probably be reluctant to slash their military spending until they were assured that their ad-versaries would make similar cuts. The Jordanians know this; they do not see their proposal as an alternative to arms control negotiations. Rather, they view the arms-for-debt swap as an incentive to encourage and facilitate arms control negotiations. The economic rewards the Jor-danian proposal holds out should expedite all phases of the arms control process.

First, an arms-for-debt swap could encourage states to launch arms control negotiations sooner rather than later. The opportunity to reduce debt and speed up economic development would help surmount the current tendency for states to "wait and see" whether they might enter such talks later in a more advantageous position. Then, once talks were under way, the allure of debt reduction could encourage negotiators to be more sincere and expeditious. They would be driven to be flexible and reach agreements quickly, not to use talks as a bargaining chip in conflict resolution or as a forum for airing grievances.

Economic incentives may even facilitate the implementation of arms control agreements. Financial technocrats, civilian ministers, business-men—indeed, any group with a stake in economic development—would share an interest in enforcing adherence to arms control arrangements. For example, given a good incentive, these groups would strive to collect more accurate information than is now available on the size and pattern of military spending.

Moreover, economic incentives may increase the constituency for arms control. If Jordan and just a few other states agreed to an arms-for-debt proposal, their economies would soon show tangible benefits. Their example could encourage citizens of Jordan's neighbors to demand similar privileges. In turn, this change in popular sentiment could expand the number and influence of officials who advocate arms control. At the very least, such pressure would strengthen the hands of those financial technocrats who already favor diversion of some military funds into development investments. An arms-for-debt initiative would build upon and encourage already existing economic pressures for arms control.

Nevertheless, economic incentives alone cannot ensure the success of arms control negotiations. They do not dictate any particular pattern of arms reductions or prescribe any specific formula for arms control. There is no royal road to demilitarization: diverse political and military issues still have to be addressed. States must still sort out their essential requirements for defense: they must identify the most threatening features of their adversaries' militaries, agree upon equivalent reductions, and erect a system of risk-minimizing verification. The process is bound to be long and agonizing. But economic incentives could greatly expedite the process. They could help pull contending states to the negotiating table and make them more forthcoming once they were there.

Regional Security Proposals

Of course, one type of state in the region may prove impervious to the inducements of arms-for-debt swaps: the oil-rich monarchies of the Gulf. Although in the aftermath of the Gulf War these countries are poorer than they once were, they are unlikely to need relief in our lifetime. Yet these states are among the least secure in the region, so they too have been eagerly searching for cheaper, more reliable ways of bolstering their defenses.

After the Gulf War, the leaders of the Gulf states rushed to form new regional alliances based on the logic of collective security.[54] Under collective security arrangements, several independent states pool their finances, manpower, and weapons to form a common front to deter or challenge aggression against any single member. In the Gulf, such formulas appeal because leaders understand that if they do not hang together they will certainly hang separately. Another attractive feature of collective security arrangements is that pooling resources for defense may be cheaper than mounting defenses individually.

The Iraqi invasion of Kuwait heightened the fears of the Gulf monarchies that their wealth made them good targets for their poorer neighbors. Individually, these states lacked the population necessary to muster armies large enough to stand up to aggressive neighbors. Even if these states had chosen to conscript *all* males reaching draft age, their armies would still have been smaller than those of their poorer neighbors (table 4-2). Clearly, these countries had strong incentives to band together for protection.

In 1981 Saudi Arabia, Kuwait, Bahrain, Qatar, the United Arab Emirates, and Oman joined together to form the Gulf Cooperation Council (GCC). Although the GCC had long discussed the virtues of military cooperation, the only steps it took in this direction were the formation of a common air defense network and the creation of a token (7,000-man) joint force called Peninsula Shield. In the aftermath of the Gulf War, however, it contemplated a far more extensive military alliance. At a meeting in Masqat in August 1991, the Omanis proposed that the GCC fund the formation of a 100,000-man joint force equipped with the most modern weapons.[55]

After the Gulf War, the GCC states also considered a proposal to extend the principle of collective security by entering a military alliance with some of the poorer countries that had joined them in the coalition against Iraq. The Egyptians and Syrians offered, in effect, to task part of their large military machines to defend the Gulf states in exchange for cash subventions. (Nuri al-Sa'id, prime minister of Iraq in the 1950s, reportedly said, "You cannot buy an Arab—but you can rent one.") In March 1991 representatives of the GCC states, Egypt, and Syria met and signed a pact known as the Damascus Declaration.[56] Under this agreement, Egypt and Syria agreed to supply several thousand troops that would form the nucleus of a pan-Arab peacekeeping force in the Gulf. In exchange for this protection, the GCC states agreed to deposit $10 billion in a development fund that Cairo and Damascus could draw upon.[57]

The Gulf states viewed the pan-Arab force envisioned in the Damascus Declaration less as a military shield than as a political umbrella. A few thousand troops strewn among the dunes might not physically block invasion, but they would remind potential aggressors that Egypt

Table 4-2. Military Manpower of the Gulf Cooperation Council States and Neighbors, 1991–92

Country	Population	Males aged 18–22	Size of armed forces
Bahrain	498,600	20,400	7,450
Kuwait	2,097,800	94,700	8,200
Oman	1,540,600	69,600	30,400
Qatar	437,400	17,800	7,500
Saudi Arabia	10,600,000	473,500	131,500
United Arab Emirates	1,708,600	55,600	44,000
GCC total	16,883,000	731,600	229,050
Egypt	56,018,000	2,623,800	420,000
Iran	53,766,400	2,658,600	528,000
Iraq	19,854,600	945,400	382,500
Syria	12,784,800	627,800	404,000
Yemen (N)	11,500,000	473,600	65,000

Source: International Institute for Strategic Studies, *The Military Balance, 1991–92* (London: Brassey's, 1991), pp. 102–23.

and Syria still stood ready to come to the defense of the oil kingdoms. Their presence would attest that the coalition that had prevailed in Operation Desert Storm might again be assembled. A small pan-Arab force would act as a reminder that a much larger force, including troops from the United States and Europe, might be summoned if needed.

Cooperation with Western militaries, rather than with other Gulf or Arab states, was the form of collective security that most interested GCC leaders. They believed the Gulf War had demonstrated that no coalition of Arab forces could be as militarily effective or as politically reliable as the security umbrella offered by the United States and other Western powers. As allied troops assembled in preparation for Operation Desert Storm, many Gulf states that had previously rejected foreign bases quietly opened their military facilities to American forces.[58] Once the Americans were victorious, these states concluded agreements giving Washington more lasting access. American bases in Oman were expanded, and Bahrain and the United Arab Emirates offered facilities to ensure that American troops would rotate in and out of their countries regularly.[59] The Kuwaitis, of course, were the most desperate for U.S. protection. Even before the liberation of Kuwait they had urged Washington to contemplate a long-term troop presence in the region, and in September 1991 they negotiated a formal security accord that called for joint exercises, training, and pre-positioning of American military equipment inside Kuwait.[60] For added safety, Kuwait signed similar accords with Great Britain and France.[61]

Taken together, these collective security measures would greatly enhance the security of the Gulf. Then–U.S. Secretary of State James Baker outlined how these arrangements should work during his testimony to Congress in September 1990.[62] Coordination among the Gulf states would allow them to pool their forces and eliminate redundancies. Stiffened by Egyptian and Syrian forces, the GCC troops would, first of all, deter attack; should deterrence fail, the troops could slow the progress of an invasion, buying time for American and European aircraft to rush to bases in the Gulf. As in Operation Desert Shield, superior air power would fend off aggressors until Western troops had assembled in numbers sufficient to overcome them.

The concept of collective security had great appeal in the Gulf, but translating that concept into practice proved difficult. The GCC states squabbled over who would control any joint military force. Some questioned the value of paying for the services of Syrian and Egyptian troops. Some shied away from granting basing rights to the Western powers. In particular, the leaders of Saudi Arabia cooled toward the idea of collective security arrangements and sought instead to build up their military power independently. While Saudi opposition did not arrest progress toward a new system of alliances in the Gulf, it certainly slowed it down.[63]

If Saudi objections can somehow be surmounted, collective security could offer a means both to make the Gulf states more secure and to retard the arms race in the region. By maintaining common forces, the Gulf states could eliminate redundant expenditures and thereby shave their individual defense budgets. (But this outcome is not certain. The experience of other collective security bodies—NATO, for one—suggests that, by pooling their resources, individual members may discover they are able to finance an even larger, more modern force.) Moreover, collective security arrangements could make arms control agreements easier to negotiate. Collective security schemes, even more than bilateral alliances, band individual states into political-military teams that can, among other things, assume a common stance during arms control talks. In arms control, as in any negotiating process, the fewer the number of contending parties, the easier it is to achieve final agreement. Moreover, protected by the umbrella of collective security, states engaged in arms control talks may feel safe enough to make bold proposals or to accept moderately risky compromises.

What Will Work?

Like economic incentive programs, such as the arms-for-debt swap, collective security schemes can help create conditions that make arms control negotiations plausible. In some ways, this is precisely what the Middle East needs. Middle Easterners already have a large menu of arms control recipes to choose from. The proliferation of weapons of mass destruction in the region might be curbed by emulating the Australia Group and restricting the production of chemical weapons; adopting the Missile Technology Control Regime; extending and expanding the Treaty on the Non-Proliferation of Nuclear Weapons; or emulating the Treaty of Tlatelolco, which banned nuclear weapons in Latin America. The threat of conventional warfare might be curbed by confidence-building measures such as intelligence exchanges and advance notification of military maneuvers; by controls on the deployment of troops and weapons, such as "limited forces zones" along borders; or even by agreements to ban or to limit the total number of specific weapons systems each state maintains. Local and international experts have described a vast array of arms control measures that might be applied in the Middle East.[64]

What has been missing in the Middle East is not some vision of what arms control arrangements are possible but the appropriate milieu for putting them into effect. Regional security plans and economic incentive programs supply the missing ingredient. They could foster an environment in which states approach arms control talks with less fear and more favor.

The Jordanian arms-for-debt proposal appears especially promising. It could harness and focus the economic pressures that have already triggered some sincere efforts to curb the arms race in the Middle East, by holding out tangible incentives for curbing military spending and participating in arms control negotiations. Attempts to alter the psychological ambience of the region have not advanced arms control; a program to change the economic atmosphere might. After all, supportive outsiders, such as Western creditors, have more influence over the economics of the region than they do over its psychology.

CHAPTER 5

Threats to Arms Control

JORDAN, YEMEN, and most of the poorer states in the Middle East are desperate to reduce their military expenditures, so they are also eager to explore the prospects for arms control. But Jordan and Yemen are not the driving forces in the regional arms race. Their armed forces are small and import only modest quantities of second-generation weapons. Their support for arms control is helpful, but it is not likely to be decisive.

Not all states are equal; some contribute more to the regional arms race than others. The states that maintain large and potent armed forces—the ones that import weapons in volume and insist upon the latest technologies—not only drive the regional arms race: ultimately they will determine the prospects for successful arms control. The regional arms race will go on unless at least some of these states embrace arms control. Indeed, if even a few of these regional powers insist upon expanding and upgrading their militaries, interest in arms control may wane among the other states in the region.

Which are the states that have driven the regional arms race during the last decade? Most experts point to six countries that maintain massive militaries, import large volumes of arms, or deploy very high-technology weaponry. These six states are the largest arms importers in the region: Iraq, Saudi Arabia, Iran, Syria, Egypt, and Israel (see table 5-1). If these six states are amenable to arms control, resistance by smaller states will not matter much. Conversely, if some of these six states decide to escalate their military development, that action will provoke a response from other states in the region. The odds for arms control depend upon how many of the six are interested, how many are benignly neutral, and how many are opposed.

Some of these states, as already suggested, now pose fewer obstacles to regional arms control arrangements than at any time in their recent

Table 5-1. Countries That Drive the Arms Race in the Middle East

Country	Arms imports, 1984–88 (billions of U.S. dollars)	Total armed forces, 1990 (thousands)	Mean years of schooling per citizen (1980)
Iraq	29.7	1,000	4.0
Saudi Arabia	19.5	67	2.7
Iran	10.5	504	3.5
Syria	8.3	404	3.0
Egypt	6.4	450	1.7
Israel	6.1	141[a]	8.8

Sources: U.S. Arms Control and Disarmament Agency, *World Military Expenditures and Arms Transfers, 1989* (1990), p. 9; International Institute for Strategic Studies, *The Military Balance, 1990–91* (London: Brassey's, 1990), pp. 102–18; and UN Development Programme, *Human Development Report, 1991* (Oxford University Press, 1991), pp. 128, 129, 174.

a. Unlike reserve units in other Middle Eastern armies, which can be mobilized only for a protracted conflict, Israel's reserve forces are highly trained and well equipped and can enter combat on short notice. In effect, these reserve units add another 504,000 soldiers to Israel's armed forces.

history. The Gulf War reduced the size of Iraq's armed forces, imposed UN inspection of its weapons industries, and left Baghdad with few funds to finance rearmament. Economic problems and the growing power of fiscal technocrats have also reduced the size of Syria's military budget. Egypt, a large but poor country whose arms imports are paid for almost entirely by military aid from the United States, has long favored arms control talks.

The other three states—Israel, Iran, and Saudi Arabia—pose special problems.[1] Israel possesses the most technologically advanced arsenal in the region; as it acquires new weapons, a half-dozen Arab states are compelled to follow suit. Many states feel menaced by Iran's Islamic revolution. Finally, Saudi Arabia's hefty cash reserves allow it to spend more on weapons than any other Middle Eastern state does. The co-operation or resistance of these states will go a long way toward promoting or souring the prospects for arms control in the region. The problems and possibilities posed by each must be examined in detail.

Israel

Israel, the most technologically advanced and militarily potent state in the region,[2] plays a unique role in the arms races that afflict the region. Israelis are convinced that a single battlefield defeat would threaten the very existence of their state, so traditionally they have been willing to bear great economic sacrifices to maintain an enormous margin of military superiority over their Arab adversaries. Israeli military doctrine has been rooted in the objective of not only defeating any imaginable coalition of Arab states, but mustering enough offensive power to preempt an attack and carry the battle onto its neighbor's territory.[3] Alone among the states in the region, Israel possesses nuclear weapons and a fully developed capacity for advanced conventional warfare. The scope of Israel's fears and the magnitude of its military requirements have made the country an unlikely candidate for arms control. Worse, Israel's quest for absolute military superiority over its neighbors has often provoked arms buildups in Arab states.

Yet in Israel, too, strong economic incentives for curbing the arms race are at work. Although the Israeli economy is both more developed than that of any Arab state and less vulnerable to variations in petroleum prices, it has become mired in an economic morass that curiously resembles that afflicting its neighbors. Thanks to the same dirigiste economic mismanagement that prevails in the Arab world, growth in the Israeli economy has been sluggish for the past ten years.[4] State subsidies, which help to keep inefficient enterprises afloat, consume $5.5 billion a year, or 10 percent of GNP—a larger share than is spent for defense. Taxes devour 56 percent of earnings and dampen incentives for investment.[5] Despite a painful stabilization program in 1985, in 1992 inflation was running more than 20 percent and unemployment, which stood at 10 percent, was projected to rise to 16 percent by 1996.[6]

Years of mismanagement has left the Israeli economy struggling under a mountain of debt. The Histradut sick fund, which provided health insurance for most Israelis, had a debt of almost $1 billion in 1991. The kibbutzim (farm collectives) had borrowed over $4 billion, which they could not repay. Israel's pension funds had an actuarial deficit of nearly $9 billion.[7] The banking system was not expected to be able to repay the government $7 billion it had borrowed during the 1983–84 financial crisis.[8] The government itself was, of course, the largest borrower. The ratio of its foreign debt to GNP stood at 30 percent in 1991 and was slated to grow to 47 percent by 1996.[9]

A new problem threatens to add significantly to Israel's debt burden: the assimilation of up to one million Jews who were expected to emigrate from the Soviet Union by 1995. The Israeli government estimates that the cost of absorbing each immigrant is around $50,000, for a total cost of around $50 billion, roughly the equivalent of one year's gross domestic product. Israel hopes to raise $18 billion toward this sum through foreign aid and credits, including $10 billion in loans guaranteed by the United States.[10]

This presents an enormous challenge to Israeli officials, who have been considering fairly radical programs to raise the money needed to absorb the Soviet immigrants. The finance minister, Yitzhak Moda'i, has proposed that Israel offer to reduce and then terminate American economic assistance over eight years—if Washington would agree to loan guarantees.[11] In 1991 the Israeli treasury launched a massive privatization drive, hoping to raise billions of dollars by selling most of its 161 state-owned enterprises.[12] Within the government there has been a growing consensus about the need to liberalize the economy, both to foster private initiative and to curb the waste and subsidies that encouraged enterprises to amass debt rather than to produce.[13] Of course, it is much easier to describe the desiderata of economic policy than it is to implement change. For any of these plans to work, Israel would have to reduce state spending drastically—including the defense budget.

Even some of the Israeli military's staunchest partisans began to argue that Israel could not afford its current level of spending. Shimon Peres, a former prime minister and minister of defense, wrote: "In our case, defense needs are growing, while the economy is not. Any growth indicated in statistics is one of consumption, not exports. Without serious economic growth, it is doubtful whether we can assure to a reasonable degree the new defense requirements."[14] Israel's troubled economy had not permitted a real increase in defense spending during the 1980s. In real terms, the annual defense budget declined from $7 billion in 1981 to $5.9 billion in 1991.[15] Although Washington supplied $1.8 billion in military assistance each year, the value of American aid since the mid-1980s had remained constant while the average cost of weapons procurement had risen 34.3 percent.[16] Israel also received $1.2 billion annually in economic aid from the United States, but this sum was entirely consumed servicing military debts to Washington.[17]

In 1990 the Israeli treasury began a concerted campaign to reduce the military budget. It began by shaving $37 million from defense appropriations, which triggered a series of bureaucratic battles over the military budget reminiscent of those occurring in Syria, albeit more public.[18] In 1991 the treasury tried to cut the defense budget by $400 million.[19] The military replied with a drive to get its budget increased by $500 million a year through 1995. The cabinet initially approved half of this sum, and then, facing fiscal pressures, slashed that allocation by 20 percent.[20] While the debate raged, certain military projects began to run out of funds, forcing the Israeli defense ministry to pay expensive contract cancellation penalties and legal fees.[21]

The Israeli chief of staff, General Ehud Barak, argued that the military needed more funding to adapt to the new style of warfare that had been demonstrated in the Gulf War. His top priorities were to increase Israel's arsenal of precision-guided munitions, to develop the Arrow antiballistic missile for protection from Scud attacks, and to launch a series of intelligence satellites to provide early warning of Arab attacks.[22] He recognized that even the maximum economically feasible increase in the defense budget would not cover these expenses, so he devised a five-year military reconfiguration plan to slash the military's spending in many areas. He canceled funding for most journals published by the Israel Defense Forces (IDF) and closed its popular radio station, reduced the number of IDF maneuvers and the size of munitions stockpiles, and contemplated mothballing tanks and aircraft. He unveiled a schedule for curbing the military's manpower demands by laying off 4,000 non-combat personnel, reducing the size of command staff by 10–20 percent, and cutting in half the number of days reservists were required to spend on active military duty.[23] His spokesman announced, "Whatever doesn't fire, will be cut. Any organization, any branch, in the IDF which is not part of the fighting forces should expect to be cut."[24]

Even these economy measures, however, cannot free up enough funds to allow Israel to pioneer new weapons systems and to absorb the Soviet immigrants. For political reasons, Israeli leaders cannot restrict the flow of immigrants. But if billions of dollars in new funds are not found, absorbing the immigrants will wreak havoc with the Israeli economy and make it difficult to sustain the defense budget or any other expenditure. Inevitably, the Israeli military will be asked to defer its spending and make additional cuts.

Under these circumstances, regional arms control arrangements may appear increasingly attractive to Israeli leaders, and an arms-for-debt swap particularly so. Consider the benefits of a swap arranged under the same terms described in table 4-1. First, by curbing its military expenditures by 20 percent of the 1987 total, Israel would release $1.2 billion annually. Second, if this cut were sustained, Israel's entire foreign debt could be written off in a little under eleven years, which would gradually release an additional $3 billion paid out now in annual debt service.[25] The $1.2 billion that Israel receives as economic aid from the United States, which now goes toward servicing military debts, could at last be spent on what it was intended to support: development.

The savings from reduced military expenditures and forgiven debt service would eventually provide Israel with $4.2 billion each year—a larger sum than the $2.0 billion in annual loans that Israel has asked Washington to guarantee. This $4.2 billion would be a cash saving, not a new loan requiring yet more debt service payments. Indeed, by liquidating its current debt, Israel would improve its credit standing, permitting it to raise additional funds on the commercial market if necessary. Equally important, raising new funds through a debt swap would encourage fiscal discipline, unlike loan guarantees from Washington, which offer a tempting opportunity for reckless public spending.[26]

There is no guarantee, of course, that Israeli generals will accede quietly to the spending cuts required by such a deal. Like Arab generals, they will be reluctant to curb their arms acquisitions unless they are assured of comparable cuts by their adversaries. But the economic incentives for agreeing to such cuts are strong on both sides. (Israel may find it easier, if anything, to implement military spending cuts: the studies that undergirded General Barak's plan for military reconfiguration have already pinpointed where the cuts might be made most safely.) Arab leaders seeking cheaper strategies of national security may well be surprised by Israeli openness to arms control proposals.

Iran

Many Arabs consider Iran, like Israel, to be a major military threat. With more than 55 million citizens, Iran is the second most populous country in the region. Iran's large oil reserves have allowed it to finance industrial and scientific development at a level much higher than the Arab norm. Since the revolution of 1979, Arab leaders have worried that Iran's call for a return to Islam could trigger subversive movements within their own countries. Even before 1979, they worried that Iran's strategic and territorial ambitions in the Gulf would clash with their own interests.

Yet over the last decade, the Iranian economy suffered a greater decline of national production than any other state in the region. In the late 1970s Iran appeared to be on the verge of becoming an NIC (newly industrialized country), and the Shah had plans to make his state a regional superpower by the year 2000. Then came the 1979 revolution, which inevitably disrupted production, triggered a flight of technically skilled personnel, and inaugurated a decade of indecision about basic economic policy. In 1980 Iraq invaded Iran, precipitating eight years of war. Tehran paid even more during the course of this war than Baghdad did, perhaps $644 billion—almost ten times the value of the 1978 GNP—and this estimate does not include the effects of wartime inflation and the loss of services of several hundred thousand of the war's casualties, or the opportunity costs of delaying investment in education and development.[27] Finally, in the mid-1980s Iran had to weather the same dramatic decline in oil prices that afflicted other Middle Eastern exporters. Together these forces pushed Iran's real gross domestic product down from $6,052 per capita in 1977 to $2,944 in 1988.[28]

By 1990, then, the Iranians found themselves facing many of the same economic problems that troubled the Iraqis. For this very reason, foreign observers—particularly Arabs—feared that Tehran might follow Baghdad's example, that is, use aggressive foreign policy to compensate for economic deficiencies.[29] The Iranians, indeed, had better reasons than Saddam to eye the wealth of the Arab Gulf states with envy and resentment. By bankrolling Iraq and summoning an American flotilla (Operation Earnest Will), the Gulf Cooperation Council had helped to force Iran to sue for peace. Gulf Arabs worried that in the respite of peace Iran would strive to rebuild its armies and then pursue its grudges militarily.

Most Iranians, however, saw their situation differently. Although the Iran-Iraq war had cost Tehran dearly, Tehran's economic situation was not as dire as Baghdad's. When the fighting ended in 1988, Iran, which had financed its war effort internally, owed $6 billion in foreign debts, compared to more than $70 billion owed by Baghdad. As a major oil exporter, Iran was still creditworthy; most officials in Tehran thought they could borrow money abroad for economic reconstruction, obviating resort to foreign policy adventurism. Indeed, to gain access to foreign credit, investment, and technology, the Islamic Republic's leaders understood they would have to avoid any moves that might alarm the West. To clear the way for improved economic relations, they sought to resolve outstanding disputes such as the disposition of Iranian assets impounded after the 1979 revolution and the seizure of foreign hostages by pro-Iranian terrorists in Lebanon.[30]

Even those Iranian leaders who could not bring themselves to endorse an "opening to the West" for economic purposes concurred that Iran's strategic position was too weak to sustain an aggressive foreign policy. In 1990 the Islamic Republic possessed only 500 tanks and 185 combat aircraft (and most of the latter were inoperable because of a shortage of spare parts), compared with 5,500 tanks and 689 combat aircraft deployed by Iraq.[31] With only these forces, Iran could not be certain it could defend itself effectively, much less attack other Gulf states. Moreover, diplomatically Iran was relatively isolated while the Arab Gulf states enjoyed a security umbrella provided by the United States and other major powers.

This configuration of forces led a minority in Tehran to argue that rebuilding the military "to defend the revolution" should be Iran's top priority. But Iran, unlike Iraq, was not an absolute dictatorship; there was lively competition among political factions. A majority of Iranian leaders, led by Ali Akbar Hashemi Rafsanjani, asserted that economic reconstruction deserved first claim on the nation's resources and favored a much smaller and gradual investment in the military. Between 1989 and 1992, this "pragmatic" or "economy-first" faction steadily edged its "revolutionary" opponents out of power.

In 1989 Hashemi Rafsanjani secured authorization from the Iranian Majlis (parliament) for his government to resume normal trade ties and to borrow funds from the West. Over the following year, he purged many of the revolutionary ideologues from Iran's economic ministries and replaced them with American-trained technocrats. These technocrats, like their Arab counterparts, saw military spending as economic waste:

> Mohammad Hossein Adeli, Iran's [Berkeley-trained] Central Bank governor, says Iran is in the process of demilitarizing its economy, shifting crucial funds from the armed forces to broader social needs. "Fortunately," he says, "we don't have any serious military threat. The threat we do have is economic. If you don't have enough food, even if you have the most sophisticated tank, how are you going to use it?"[32]

Similar sentiments were common in the Majlis: one deputy proposed that 10 percent of the defense budget be set aside "to create recreational and cultural centers for young people."[33] In January 1990 the Majlis approved Rafsanjani's $394 billion five-year plan for economic reconstruction, which projected $119 billion of hard currency investment, including $27 billion of foreign borrowing.[34]

The five-year plan exemplified a new, more liberal, approach to economic and foreign policy that was supported not only by Iran's political elite but, to all appearances, by the Iranian populace. By 1991 economic issues were paramount among concerns of average Iranians: inflation was running at more than 50 percent, strikes by wageworkers had become commonplace, and demonstrations against price rises had triggered serious violence.[35] In the April–May 1992 Majlis elections, Rafsanjani and his "economy-first" allies swept the balloting, driving their most important revolutionary opponents completely out of the assembly.[36]

Pragmatists in the Iranian leadership assigned low priority to military spending, but this did not mean they favored disarmament. Iran had to defend 1,000 miles of border abutting Central Asia's tumultuous republics, a 900-mile border against Iraq, and a 1,000-mile coastline facing the Arab Gulf states. Iran's new foreign policy sought to improve relations along all these borders by stabilizing relations with Iraq, offering assistance to the Central Asian republics, and even petitioning for inclusion in collective security arrangements with the Arab Gulf states.[37] To ensure that these borders remained peaceful, however, Tehran began gradually to repair and upgrade its armed forces.

In June 1989 Iran signed a multiyear arms deal with Moscow whose total value may have been as much as $5 billion.[38] As the Soviet Union dissolved, new arms agreements were concluded with the individual republics of the Commonwealth of Independent States, and with China and North Korea.[39] The Iranians seem to have been particularly eager to rebuild their air force; the bulk of the arms funds was earmarked for importing fighters and bombers. Between 1990 and 1992 Tehran received at least twenty MIG-29 fighters, a dozen Sukhoi-24 fighter-bombers, and around fifty other combat aircraft. But there were reports that Iran was also buying 200–250 T-72 tanks, Scud surface-to-surface missiles, and three diesel-powered submarines.[40]

In January 1992 CIA Director Robert Gates testified before Congress that "Iran has embarked on an across-the-board effort to develop its military and defense industries."[41] CIA estimates suggested that Iran planned to spend up to $2 billion each year through 1994 on arms imports.[42] Some pundits in Washington and the Gulf began to portray

Iran as a major weapons proliferator and a threat to stability in the Middle East.

But many experts dissent. They note that Iran's defense budget in 1991 was 413 billion rials. At the official exchange rate this sum was $5.9 billion, but at the free market rates it amounted to only $295 million. Even assuming that Tehran's defense ministry received most of its budget in hard currency, the figure is not especially alarming—the Shah spent much more on the military. The constant (1988) dollar value of Iranian military spending had declined from over $12 billion in 1981 to $5 billion in 1990.[43] Defense spending at $5.9 billion a year would equal 10 percent of GDP—a low figure by regional standards. Some authorities, such as the Institute for International Strategic Studies in London, estimate that in 1991 Iran spent only $3.7 billion on defense.[44]

Many military analysts are not anxious about the arsenal Iran is acquiring. They note that, with jet fighters costing $20–$25 million each and submarines $250 million each, Iran's $2 billion arms import budget is not large enough to create a force that threatens its neighbors:

> After massive losses of men and equipment in the Iran-Iraq war, Iran must rebuild "almost from ground zero," one envoy [in Tehran] said. Despite the devastation of Iraq's armed forces during the gulf war last year, Iraq's army is still vastly superior to that of Iran. Iran's air force is still largely composed of American-made aircraft that have lacked spare parts and maintenance since the time of the Shah, and its navy has improved little since the 1979 revolution. "Reports of Iran's military buildup are highly exaggerated," said one foreign envoy in Teheran who spends all of his time analyzing Iran's military. "Iran is not doing more than what it should be doing for its legitimate self-defense." Said another envoy: "For what Iran needs to rebuild, $2 billion a year is peanuts."[45]

Some analysts doubt that Iran can sustain even a $2 billion annual budget for arms imports. Iran's oil exports are worth $15 billion annually, and domestic hard currency needs are around $25 billion.[46]

Iran cannot be, then, a driving force in the Middle East arms race at the moment. True, it is also unlikely to be an enthusiastic advocate of arms control. With only $10 billion in foreign debt, most of it recently acquired from commercial banks, Iran is not an ideal candidate for an arms-for-debt swap. But if Tehran may not contribute much to abetting arms control, neither is it likely to do much to hinder it, because regional arms control arrangements are likely to leave Iran more secure. Also,

Iran is eager to curry goodwill in the West and in the Gulf, and it takes a keen interest in any proposals for regional collective security arrangements. If the Arabs can launch a serious arms control project, they may find Iranian collaboration forthcoming.

Saudi Arabia

Most Arabs think Israel is responsible for the arms race in the Middle East. The Bush administration blames Iran. It is natural and understandable that leaders tend to blame the arms race on their enemies, but sometimes the blame is misplaced. Ironically, the most active arms proliferator in the region today—Saudi Arabia—has largely escaped opprobrium.

During the 1980s Saudi Arabia was the largest single buyer on the international arms market, consuming $46.7 billion worth of weapons.[47] In the aftermath of the Gulf War, the Saudis launched plans to triple their arms spending. During the 1990s Saudi Arabia's orgy of weapons acquisitions may be the most potent single threat to the prospects for Middle Eastern arms control.

Within a year of the allied victory over Iraq, plans for collective security in the Gulf began to collapse. Several factors led to this failure, including disagreements among the GCC states over whom to include, how much to fund, and how to distribute authority over any joint command emerging from a new security arrangement.[48] But the most decisive obstacle to security cooperation was the dramatic shift in the military strategy of Saudi Arabia.

The taproot of Saudi resistance to collective security lay in domestic politics. One of the foundations of Saudi rule was the dynasty's imposition of an intellectual quarantine on their country: the regime strictly controlled travel by Saudi subjects abroad; the import of films, books, and magazines; and any other form of intercourse that might have allowed alien ideas to infiltrate the kingdom. The quarantine inhibited the spread of threatening ideas—such as democracy, equality, and popular sovereignty—among the Saudi population. It also pleased the ulama, the reactionary religious scholars who acted as the dynasty's ideological police, because it dampened the spread of "lewd pictures of women" and "atheistic science" that might undermine belief in fundamentalist Islam.[49]

The presence of large numbers of foreign troops on Saudi soil, or in the neighboring Gulf states, threatened to breach the quarantine. During the Gulf War, allied troops had been carefully stationed in the desert— far from Saudi population centers—and the imposition of elaborate rules of etiquette had minimized the possibility that they would infect the Saudis with their ideas.[50] Despite the precautions, the mere presence of Western troops on Saudi soil bred dissent. Saudi journalists, emboldened by CNN and other media newly admitted to the country, began to test the limits of state censorship.[51] The Kingdom's most oppressed minority, the Shi'is, became more assertive.[52] Its most oppressed majority, women, were heartened when seventy women staged a public protest in downtown Riyadh against a law banning women from driving automobiles.[53] Stirred by these developments, forty-three Saudi liberals drew up a petition "asking King Fahd for a consultative assembly, modernization of the legal system and controls on the *mutawa.*"[54]

The ring of demands for change elicited a forceful reaction from the Right, which was appalled by the liberalizing tendencies brought by foreign troops into the kingdom.[55] To the surprise and horror of the dynasty, in May 1991 more than four hundred ulama signed their own petition to the king, demanding their own voice in government (including the right to approve cabinet selections); a purging of "state bodies of anyone convicted of corruption or negligence"; and a "rebuilding [of] the media and all their services in accordance with the information policy adopted by the Kingdom to serve Islam, express society's morals, and enhance its culture."[56] The ulama, who had growing support inside the Kingdom's military, also rejected any security arrangements that might threaten further ideological "pollution" of society. They advised the king to keep the country "out of non-Islamic pacts and treaties," to diversify its sources of arms, and to build up Saudi Arabia's own armed forces.[57]

Over the following year, the conservative movement expanded its criticisms, adding a stinging critique of Saudi participation in the Middle Eastern peace process. It grew steadily in strength and obtained a series of important concessions from the Crown.[58] The attendant political controversy confirmed the royal family's conviction that the conservatives were right about one thing: using foreign troops to protect the kingdom threatened the regime's security more than it bolstered it. This conclusion reinforced the dynasty's decision to expand its armed forces and to rely more on them than on collective security arrangements for defense.

The Sauds made their first moves toward increasing the size of their military immediately after Iraq invaded Kuwait. King Fahd announced plans to expand the armed forces, called for the formation of a volunteer force to meet Iraqi aggression, and, for the first time, asked for the power to impose military conscription. A training program was established to prepare all university graduates for military service—a revolutionary move, since it meant setting aside traditional recruitment along tribal lines.[59] Plans were drafted to increase the size of the regular army from 38,000 to 80,000–90,000.[60] The Saudi National Guard, which recruited largely from the Bedouin and had performed better than the regular army during the Gulf War, was also to be reorganized along American lines and expanded. Together these measures would triple the size of the Saudi armed forces, giving the Kingdom around 200,000 troops.[61]

Of course, these troops would be armed with the very best weapons money could buy. Riyadh wanted to acquire all of the wonder weapons whose blistering effectiveness the Americans had demonstrated during Operation Desert Storm. This included the "big five" American weapons systems: the M1 Abrams main battle tank, the M2 Bradley infantry fighting vehicle, the UH-60 Black Hawk transport helicopter, the AH-64 Apache attack helicopter, and the Patriot air defense missile.[62] Immediately after the Gulf War, Riyadh presented Washington with orders for $23.5 billion in weapons for its ground forces alone.[63] The Saudis were also planning to double the size of their air force and hoped to spend $4 billion for seventy-two F-15 fighter planes.[64]

The purchase of big-ticket weapons systems, however, was perhaps not the most significant element of Riyadh's military expansion plans. The Saudi officers, like their peers across the Arab world, had studied the performance of American forces in Operation Desert Storm with awe. They saw that the Americans themselves attributed much of their victory to the effectiveness of new high-technology weapons that performed three missions: "communications, command, control and intelligence; defense suppression; and precision guidance."[65] Space satellite systems, airborne reconnaissance planes (such as AWACS and JSTARS), night vision equipment, and navigational aids (such as global positioning satellites) allowed the allies to pinpoint Iraqi targets and maximize the firepower directed against them. Stealth attack bombers, cruise missiles, and diverse electronic countermeasures enabled the allies to cripple Iraqi radar and communications facilities. Precision-guided weapons, including the notorious "smart bombs," "standoff" missiles, and multiple-launch rocket vehicles, permitted devastatingly accurate allied attacks. These three types of technology inaugurated a new style of warfare: advanced conventional weapons enabled a commander to demolish an opponent's communications, leaving enemy troops paralyzed or uncoordinated and exposed to withering air attacks.[66]

The Saudis were determined to acquire these high-technology weapons and to enter the era of advanced conventional warfare. In August 1991 they spent $365 million buying assorted sophisticated bombs and missiles, including 2,000 Mk-84 aircraft bombs, 2,100 CBU-87 cluster munitions, and 770 AIM-7 Sparrow air-to-air missiles from Washington.[67] By September they had also concluded an agreement giving them access to American global positioning system satellites.[68] They already possessed one of the most advanced aerial reconnaissance systems in the region and were eager to expand it further.[69]

The decision to acquire all this leading-edge hardware and to build up the largest military force in the Gulf led to important changes in Saudi foreign policy. Riyadh became more assertive and less inclined to accommodate the demands of other regional powers than before the war. James Akins, former American ambassador to the Kingdom, described well the growth of Saudi Arabia's ambitions when he wrote:

> Riyadh is determined that Saudi Arabia, not Iran, will dominate the gulf in the Postwar era. If the Saudis do not unify the GCC under their flag, they will be its unquestioned dominant power; never again will the smaller states defy Saudi Arabia on border issues or on oil quotas in OPEC. Furthermore, Saudi Arabia will be the Arab Sparta, the Arab Israel. It will train and arm its own army; it will buy the world's most sophisticated weaponry; it will keep the Americans on hand to give support when needed. The Kingdom may take a step or two toward representative government, but the Saudi people will be kept satisfied by growing prosperity. Any opposition to the American presence from religious fundamentalists and the few who still entertain broader Arab nationalist views can be bought off. Everyone has his price.[70]

This change from the Kingdom's traditional policy of appeasement toward its neighbors had profound effects on the evolution of regional security arrangements.

First, Riyadh became much less supportive of—and in some cases hostile to—collective security schemes. The Saudis did not want to divert funds from their own military to the creation of a large GCC joint force, nor were they interested in creating an army that might encourage the autonomy of their smaller neighbors. At the December 1991 GCC summit, Saudi opposition helped kill the Omani plan for a 100,000-man joint force.[71] Moreover, the Saudis, convinced that their own military could provide a more-than-adequate tripwire against Iraqi or Iranian aggression, showed little enthusiasm for the Damascus Declaration. After all, basing Egyptian or Syrian troops on the peninsula presented the same threat of ideological infection as importing American troops— only the danger was Arabist rather than liberal ideology. While the Saudis stood by, the Damascus Declaration fell apart over wrangling between Egypt and Kuwait on the price of Cairo's support.[72]

Riyadh's new assertiveness even led to problems in coordinating security arrangements with the Americans. In the aftermath of the Gulf War, the American military had expected that it would be able to rotate planes and ships regularly into Saudi bases and would be able to pre-position enough military supplies in the Kingdom to outfit at least a division.[73] Instead, the Saudis refused to permit stationing of American troops, resisted pre-positioning, and declined to sign a "status-of-force" memorandum that would have defined the American military's rights of access in the kingdom.[74] Riyadh's recalcitrance did not mean that the Saudis thought they could dispense with American protection; no Saudi officer believed that his troops, no matter how numerous, would be able to offer the kind of security supplied by the U.S. Marine Corps. But the Saudis did believe that their own military could defend the Kingdom in an emergency until U.S. forces arrived, and they wanted to maintain control over when to summon the Americans as well as to insulate Saudi society from foreign influences.[75]

Saudi Arabia's new military assertiveness not only undercut plans for collective security in the region, it also greatly undermined hopes for cultivating areawide arms control programs. Collective security plans would have enhanced the defenses of the Gulf Arabs without requiring a major increase in the arms flow to the region. The American, Egyptian, and Syrian arsenals were already replete, and a 100,000-man GCC joint force could have been outfitted without a significant increase in the military budgets of the member states. In contrast, plans to inflate the Saudi military would not only require a massive increase in Saudi Arabia's military budget, but would trigger similar expansions in the other GCC states and stimulate arms spending throughout the region.

The smaller Arab Gulf states naturally were alarmed when Riyadh distanced itself from collective security arrangements in favor of a new vision of "Pax Saudica." Bereft of a viable collective security scheme and eager to assert their prestige and autonomy vis-à-vis Riyadh, they eagerly followed the Saudi lead and began enlarging their own armed forces. Like the Saudis, they had access to Western credit and Western arms stocks, which allowed them to go on a shopping spree despite their short-term cash flow problems. After U.S. Secretary of Defense Richard Cheney toured the Gulf states in May 1991, he returned to Washington with orders for over twenty Apache attack helicopters, almost four hundred Abrams tanks, and nearly two hundred Bradley fighting vehicles.[76] Arms procurement officials from the Gulf states swamped the Le Bourget and Dubai air shows in the fall of 1991 to bid on aircraft like the Tornado, the Eagle, and the Hornet, on helicopters such as the Gazelle and the Apache, and on munitions such as the GBU-28 "burrowing bomb."[77] Kuwait decided to double the size of its air force by buying seventy-five F/A-18 Hornet strike fighters.[78] The 1991–92 Kuwaiti budget called for a sixfold increase in defense spending, to 43.4 percent of its total budget.[79]

Abdallah Bishara, the Kuwaiti secretary general, summarized the arms-buying trend nicely: "We must have more teeth and more bite. Cash on the barrelhead will determine who gets arms."[80]

Other Middle Eastern states watched the arms buildup in the Gulf with alarm, worried that it augured a change in the style of warfare—a shift to advanced conventional weapons—that would make their own arsenals inadequate or obsolete. Israel had been working for a decade to develop an armory of advanced conventional weapons that would establish a qualitative advantage over Arab forces, which it could not match in quantity.[81] Gulf arms purchases justified demands for an upgrade and modernization of the Israeli arsenal, thereby scuttling finance ministry plans calling for a reduction of military spending.[82] Iran too seemed poised to match the Arab Gulf states by increasing its military spending.[83]

Officers in the poorer Arab states would have liked to follow suit. Of course they had observed the effectiveness of advanced conventional weapons during Operation Desert Storm. They too dreamed of upgrading their arsenals. However, for the most part they lacked the access to Western credit and armories that the Gulf states enjoyed. Still, with patience and enough time, the poorer Arab states could gradually re-equip their forces and outfit themselves for a future of advanced conventional warfare. Perhaps the most important consequence of Saudi Arabia's decision to expand its armed forces is that officers in neighboring states can thereby justify the maintenance of their own military budgets against cuts advocated by their civilian opponents. The Saudi military buildup may well trigger a new round of the Middle Eastern arms race despite the forces working to restrain it.[84]

The Possibilities for Change

The Saudi military buildup appears to be the most serious threat to regional arms control prospects, but a renewed, full-out arms race is far from inevitable.

For one thing, it is unclear whether even the oil-rich Gulf states can afford as much of an arms race as they might like. The Gulf War did not impoverish any of these countries, but it did saddle them with cash flow problems. Most of them had spent more than they could pay out of current revenues, and they were forced to liquidate assets, borrow abroad, or delay arms purchases. Although all had signed expensive new arms contracts, several encountered difficulties paying for them, which was reflected in a series of contract cancellations and deferments.

Bahrain, which was no longer a major oil exporter, had counted on financial assistance from its neighbors when it asked the United States to sell it Apache attack helicopters. When this assistance did not materialize, it had to scale back its plans and settle for cheaper Cobra helicopters.[85] Kuwait had projected ambitious purchases of new aircraft and tanks. But when the Amir tallied the cost of purchasing arms, repairing damage to the oil industry, and absorbing the bad debts of the banking system, the total came to $65 billion; the Kuwaiti government's total assets were around $80 billion. Moreover, Kuwait's $21 billion 1991 budget projected a deficit of $18 billion.[86] Rather than liquidate all the country's assets, the Kuwaitis chose to reconsider plans for expanding the military. Diplomats observed, "The military is being given a lower priority than civil reconstruction, which has meant the military has little money to commit to arms purchases."[87] To help cover the cost of new equipment, the Kuwaiti military decided to decrease the size of its forces from the pre–Gulf War levels.

Even Saudi Arabia discovered that it could not finance all its military ambitions. As early as March 1991, the Saudis asked Washington to defer consideration of some of their arms requests because of funding problems.[88] Plans to request congressional approval for a Saudi purchase of seventy-two F-15 fighter-bombers were delayed in the fall of 1991 and again in the spring of 1992 partly because of cash flow problems.[89] Saudi purchases from other powers were also affected. In 1986 the Saudis had contracted to buy forty-eight Tornado fighter-bombers and eighty-eight Black Hawk transport helicopters from Great Britain. After the Gulf War the Saudis no longer had the money to do both, so they announced they would defer the Black Hawk purchase.[90] Riyadh canceled outright a $3.17 billion deal to purchase three air-defense frigates from France.[91] The Saudi government also signaled its intention to draw on the country's private banking deposits to meet government obligations; to make a final $1.5 billion payment on its al-Yamama arms deal with Britain, Riyadh borrowed the funds from domestic banks.[92]

The financial constraints on the ability of the Gulf states to acquire advanced weapons are compounded by other problems. For instance, manpower resources are ample for the creation of modern air forces, but they severely circumscribe the size of potential ground forces (see table 4-2). Political considerations may limit the size of ground forces even further, since the Gulf dynasties historically have resisted imposing military conscription.

"No taxation, therefore no representation" has been a tenet in these monarchies. Since oil made the Gulf dynasties rich enough to rule without demanding contributions from their subjects, they have been able to treat their states as personal fiefs and have felt no need to share power. Imposing military conscription on subjects and asking them to die in defense of the nation would necessarily confer modern citizenship rights, however, and set the populace on the road to demanding a share of power.[93] Moreover, the Gulf dynasties have been reluctant to create large standing armies for fear that they—like armies in other Arab states—might edge into the business of making coups.

Another factor may inhibit the buildup of weaponry in the Gulf and the drift toward a new regional arms race: the role of the United States. Washington supplies the bulk of weapons deployed in the Gulf, and relatively minor changes in its policies often have profound effects on the regional arms race.

This was evident immediately after the Gulf War when American representatives toured Riyadh and other Gulf capitals to discuss regional security arrangements. The U.S. negotiators' mission was to examine collective security arrangements for the region, but perhaps because the American team was dominated by representatives from the Pentagon, the talks tended to focus on the prospects for pre-positioning American military equipment on the Arabian peninsula. The American team was surprised by Saudi Arabia's reluctance to tolerate "foreign influences" on its soil, even in the small numbers necessary to guard pre-positioned equipment. In an effort to sweeten the deal, the Americans offered to sell the Saudis various advanced weapons systems. By all reports, the issue of arms control never came up; if the Bush initiative had linked arms control too tightly to the peace process, it had not linked it securely enough to talks about regional security arrangements. The Americans made similar offers, rooted in the same logic, to Kuwait, Bahrain, and the United Arab Emirates.[94]

The result was an unprecedented flood of arms sales that included some of the most sophisticated weapons in the American arsenal. In fact, by February 1991 the White House had already notified Congress that it was considering $23 billion worth of weapons sales to the Middle East for that year alone.[95] Table 5-2 lists those sales concluded by the administration and approved by Congress by September 1992; many other deals were pending. Despite President Bush's assertion that "it would be tragic" if the Gulf War was followed by a renewal of the arms race in the region, the United States quickly emerged as the largest weapons seller in the Middle Eastern market.[96] Indeed, in 1991 the value of U.S. arms sales to Saudi Arabia alone exceeded the value of all Soviet arms sales to the third world.[97]

During the 1992 election campaign, President Bush lobbied hard for new arms sales to the Middle East in the hope of promoting U.S. exports and stimulating the economy. He approved the sale of 72 F-15 fighter-bombers to Saudi Arabia, a contract that would earn $9 billion and provide employment for 7,000 McDonnell Douglas workers in Oklahoma and Texas.[98] He persuaded Kuwait to buy 236 of General Dynamics' advanced M1-A2 main battle tanks, earning the firm $4 billion and preserving another 5,900 jobs.[99] In the past, Israeli resistance had obstructed similar sales to the Gulf. So, to win the acquiescence of the

Table 5-2. U.S. Arms Sales to the Middle East, August 2, 1990–September 14, 1992

Country	Weapons system	Cost (millions of U.S. dollars)
Bahrain	Tanks, reconnaissance electronics	37
Egypt	Trucks, jet fighters, advanced ammunition and bombs, surface-to-air missiles	2,170
Israel	Antiballistic missiles, jet fighters, transport helicopters	468
Kuwait	Air base upgrade, antiballistic missiles, surface-to-air missiles	2,850
Morocco	Jet fighters	250
Oman	Armored personnel carriers	150
Saudi Arabia	Jet fighters, air-to-air missiles, tanks, advanced ammunition and bombs, surface-to-air missiles, antitank missiles, reconnaissance electronics, attack helicopters, surface-to-surface rockets, tanker aircraft, tactical vehicles, antiballistic missiles, armored personnel carriers, transport aircraft	25,700
United Arab Emirates	Attack helicopters, antitank missiles, air-to-surface missiles, transport aircraft	737
Total		32,362

Source: "New World Orders: U.S. Arms Transfers to the Middle East," *Arms Control Today*, vol. 22 (September 1992), pp. 36–37.

Rabin government, the Bush administration offered to give Israel's forces attack helicopters and weapons worth $700 million from U.S. surplus inventories, to pre-position $200 million of advanced munitions inside Israel, and to collaborate more closely with Tel Aviv in the development of advanced military technologies.[100]

When queried about the scope of U.S. arm sales, American officials replied, "There is absolutely no contradiction between arms control and arms sales."[101] Perhaps this answer meant the Bush administration subscribed to the argument of those who assert that the only realistic objective of arms control is to keep America's allies stronger than its enemies. But, assuming that arms control means in Washington what it does in other capitals—efforts to curb the risks of war by curtailing the production, transfer, or deployment of weapons—perhaps the official formula was simply high hypocrisy. American arms sales deeply damaged the prospects for arms control in the region.

By cashing in on the lucrative market for weapons sales in the Middle East, the United States encouraged other powers to follow suit. The runaway arms sales doomed the talks convened by the "Big Five" arms suppliers—talks that had been meant to construct a suppliers' cartel for reducing arms transfers to the region.[102] Worse, by delivering a new generation of weapons to the oil-rich Gulf states, Washington planted the seeds for a new arms race. Neighboring countries inevitably would update their own armories when they saw the latest American weapons systems deployed on their borders.

However, there was no American consensus on the desirability of pumping large quantities of arms into the Gulf. The Pentagon tended to lobby for such sales if only because Gulf weapons orders increased the size of production runs, thereby lowering unit costs and saving the American military money. The State Department was more skeptical about the value of the arms sales, complaining that the Pentagon's official review of Saudi Arabian defense needs, which had laid out plans for the sales, had been kept so secret that State Department officials had been denied a chance to read it.[103] Congress, prodded by concern for Israel's security, had long resisted major arms transfers to the Gulf and, following the Gulf War, had even proposed a moratorium on sales to the region.[104]

A minor change in the balance of power in Washington could result in major restraints on Gulf weapons purchases. If Washington acted in concert with other weapons suppliers, the drift toward an arms race in the Gulf could be averted. Even acting unilaterally to curb the flow of arms, Washington could produce dramatic results. Gulf states might be able to buy equipment from other states, but they would not be fully satisfied: "Saudi officials often have stated they would prefer to buy American products. Not only do they regard U.S. products as technologically superior, but they appreciate the logistical support that comes with them as well as the political support they imply."[105] The last element—political support—plays a more important role in Saudi preferences than is commonly acknowledged. The Saudis and the other Gulf regimes understand that, even if they could buy all the weapons they had ever dreamed of, they would still not have an adequate defense against their neighbors. In the final analysis, the Gulf states depend on the American security umbrella. Expanding their own armed forces might deter their neighbors and it might allow them to slow a surprise attack, but their populations are too small and their political structures too fragile to fend off a major assault without support from Washington.

The Gulf regimes think of American arms purchases as a means to strengthen Washington's commitment to defend their region. In campaigns to acquire arms, they win allies in the Pentagon, among arms manufacturers, and among congressmen representing arms-producing districts. By prevailing over the protests of pro-Israel lobbyists, they demonstrate to themselves and their neighbors the depth of American interest in their survival. By employing American weapons within their territories, they believe they create an American stake in their security.[106] If they were forced to purchase non-American weapons, they would not be buying any of these perceived political benefits.

Thus, although the buildup of new weapons in the Gulf is a potential threat to the prospects for regional arms control, the threat is neither inevitable nor insurmountable. Financial difficulties, by themselves, will probably slow the arms race in the Gulf. Political action could arrest it. Like Iran's quest to rearm and Israel's search for absolute strategic superiority, the arms buildup in the Gulf is a threat mainly because it discourages policymakers from contemplating arms control.

CHAPTER 6

Conclusions

THE MIDDLE EAST is subject to one of the maxims that govern most modern states: military insecurity often overrides economic rationality. Arab leaders, like their counterparts in Washington and Moscow—not to mention in New Delhi or Havana—tend to view economic development as an elective, whereby they can choose to achieve progress by making temporary sacrifices. In contrast, they perceive military security to be a matter of life or death—not merely desirable—wherein a momentary lapse may lead to disaster. They presume their citizens will be willing to sacrifice some of the comforts of economic growth in order to ensure maximum security. Hence, that arms control may be economically rational does not ensure that it will prevail over political factors that promote the arms race.

Yet the cash-flow problems that the Middle East will face in the 1990s are so serious that most states will be forced to reduce their military expenditures; many have already done so. The money is just not there any more. And political developments reinforce the economic necessity. The prestige of the officer corps has declined in many countries because promises of military industrialization or battlefield victory have gone unfulfilled. As the fiscal problems of the region loom larger, financial technocrats who favor diverting state funds from military budgets to civilian investments have grown more influential. Most important, among the general public there is a growing sense that too much has been spent on arms and not enough on development.

Economists would say the public is developing a growing appreciation of the *opportunity cost* of the arms race, which means that to gain more of one good, one must give up some of another good. In the Middle East, the opportunity costs imposed by the arms race have been exceptionally high. The billions of dollars that local states have invested in aircraft and tanks have not improved literacy, diet, or longevity. Rather, they have bred devastating wars and debilitating foreign debts. As the economic security of the majority declines, people ask more penetrating questions about the price of current forms of military security. Middle Easterners' new willingness to challenge old assumptions about spending for the military—not the reduction of hostilities among states with long histories of injustice and aggression toward one another—is the most prominent psychological transformation in the region.

The necessity of restricting or reducing military budgets creates an unprecedented opportunity to promote arms control. Military budgets are under so much pressure that officers are often asked to trim not just fat but muscle. Since the only way to prevent such cuts from weakening a country's defenses is to match them with similar reductions among its adversaries, officers and other members of the political elite are increasingly receptive to arms control proposals. They have come to view arms control not as an alternative to military security, but as one of several strategies for obtaining it.

That the urge to restrict arsenals and extend arms control arises from the Middle Eastern states themselves is important. In the past, arms control plans for the region have revolved around the idea of creating a suppliers' cartel that would control arms exports to the region.[1] But efforts to construct a suppliers' cartel have consistently failed, and even if one could be built, its interventions would probably be counterproductive.

Economists tend to be justifiably skeptical about the merits of cartels. They note that over the long run supply-side controls do not diminish demand; they only raise prices.[2] Unless the demand for arms is also curbed, a Big-Five exporters' cartel would only raise the price of weapons in the Middle East. Higher prices, in turn, would raise the incentives for some of the industrializing countries of Eastern Europe, Latin America, and Southeast Asia to expand their weapons manufacture and to compete for a share of the lucrative Middle Eastern market.

Worse, a suppliers' cartel would dampen the political forces currently promoting arms control in the Middle East. Constituencies for arms control in the Middle East—such as the civilian ministers and financial bureaucrats who view local military spending as an excessive burden on their national budgets—are already in place. The influence of these elites would be undermined by an external cartel, since their proposals for arms control could be cast as unpatriotic collaboration with coercive foreign powers.

Incentive programs, on the other hand, would increase the size of the benefits that would follow from reduced military spending, which would bolster the arguments of local elites who favor arms control. Incentive programs link the issues of militarization and development, highlighting the opportunity costs that the arms race imposed. The Jordanian proposal is a particularly elegant incentive program, but related proposals that make economic aid, technology transfer, or access to overseas markets conditional upon arms curbs would have similar effects.[3]

Incentives can add to the number of countries interested in demilitarization, facilitate their agreement to begin arms control talks, and augment their flexibility once negotiations have begun. Arms control talks themselves will never be easy. Reconciling Israel's insistence on absolute strategic superiority with Arab demands for credible national defense will take long, hard hours of work. But both the Arabs and the Israelis have concrete proposals for arms control. They have before them a host of international agreements that might be extended to address local problems: the nuclear nonproliferation treaty, the Australia Group on chemical weapons, the Missile Technology Control Regime. Also, more radical proposals exist for enhancing security while curtailing arms acquisitions, such as plans for defensive reconfiguration or cooperative security.[4] No one can say yet which idea or combination of ideas will prove most fruitful, but incentive programs will make agreement on any of them easier to achieve.

Outside powers can play a constructive role in promoting regional arms control arrangements if they are careful to adopt tactics that reinforce rather than erode regional trends. They could, for instance, augment the incentives for arms control, not seek to impose finished arrangements. But perhaps most important, foreign powers can restrain their arms sales. The United States, by pumping a new generation of weapons into the Gulf states, has clearly not been helpful. As the glow that attended its Desert Storm victory faded, the Bush administration's initial enthusiasm for arms control was replaced by a cynical realpolitik. Policymakers in Washington apparently convinced themselves that an arms control regime need apply only to those states that were antagonistic toward the United States. They failed—or refused—to see the connection between Washington's own burgeoning arms sales and the prospects for renewal of the regional arms race.

To have any legitimacy, arms control regimes must apply to all sides of a conflict. States will accept arms control only when their opponents accept similar restraints on their military forces. By agreeing to sell billions of dollars' worth of new weapons to the oil-rich Gulf states— far more than the Iraqis, Iranians, and Syrians could possibly finance— the United States seriously undermined the prospects for arms control in the region.

Of course, it is not too late to curb the surge of American weapons flowing to the Gulf and to discourage the renewal of the regional arms race. By curbing its sales, Washington might once again take the lead in the struggle for Middle Eastern arms control. By promoting collective security arrangements among the Gulf states, it might dampen local demand for arms imports. And by endorsing incentive programs, it might foster international collaboration that would improve the prospects for peace.

But if Washington, or any other power, wishes to contribute to these trends, it must act soon. There is nothing irresistible and inevitable— much less eternal—about current trends. Once reconstruction from the damages of the Gulf War nears completion, once the assimilation of Arab workers displaced from the Gulf and Soviet Jews who migrate to Israel is largely accomplished, more funds for military spending will become available. Most petroleum economists predict that real oil prices will begin to rise by the end of the 1990s, and some fear that the rapid growth of energy demand in East Asia may lead soon to a sudden rise in prices.[5] In any case, the financial pressures that currently create an opening for arms control will not last forever.

Some threads of common culture unite the peoples of the Middle East, despite the political hostilities that divide them. One of those threads is a collection of folk stories about Sheikh Juha,[6] a medieval religious scholar and *idiot savant*, which couches moral messages in humorous terms. One of these stories may hold a lesson for arms control.

Legend has it that Juha once made a pilgrimage in the company of a Hindu ascetic and a Christian priest. One day the three travelers were surprised to discover a cake of *halawah*, a delicious dessert, lying by the side of the road. Unable to agree on how to divide this treasure, they decided to make camp and pray for divine guidance. When they awoke the next morning, each of them had had a dream that appeared to decide the issue.

The Hindu ascetic said, "The Lord Siva came to me in a dream last night. He told me that this *halawah* was a symbol of how all the goods of this world lie at the command of those who have attained enlightenment. He said that I, having practiced many austerities over the years, have now reached enlightenment and thus deserve the *halawah* most."

The Christian priest said, "I dreamed last night that Jesus appeared before me. He said that this *halawah* was a symbol of his body, which he had sacrificed to wash away man's sins. And he said that I, who had accepted him as my savior, deserve the *halawah* most."

Then Juha said, "Last night the angel Gabriel appeared to me in a dream. He said: 'Juha, eat the *halawah* now!' So I did." And, sure enough, the *halawah* was gone.

What is true of *halawah* also seems to be true of arms control. Debates about who is right and who is wrong can be pointless and endless. The best possible advice for those who hope to curb the Middle East arms race is, Do it *now*, before other visions have a chance to prevail.

Notes

CHAPTER 1

1. In this book the term *Gulf War* refers to the 1991 conflict between Iraq and the American-led coalition. The 1980–88 conflict between Baghdad and Tehran—previously called "the Gulf War"—is dubbed the Iran-Iraq war.

2. Secretary of State Baker, "Opportunities to Build a New World Order," Statement before the House Foreign Affairs Committee, U.S. Congress, Washington, D.C., February 6, 1991, in U.S. Department of State, *Dispatch*, vol. 2 (February 11, 1991), p. 810.

3. David White, "Iraq Still Has Great Numbers of Tanks," *Financial Times*, October 4, 1991, p. 4.

4. "The Race to Be Powerfullest," *The Economist*, February 9, 1991, p. 22.

5. Natalie J. Goldring, *Arms Transfers to the Middle East* (Washington: Defense Budget Project, April 25, 1991), tables 3 and 4, pp. 16, 17; and U.S. Arms Control and Disarmament Agency, *World Military Expenditures and Arms Transfers, 1989* (October 1990), pp. 7–15, 73–76.

6. Office of Technology Assessment, U.S. Congress, *Global Arms Trade: Commerce in Advanced Military Technology and Weapons*, OTA-ISC-460 (Government Printing Office, June 1991), p. 6.

7. The origin of the concept of a "new world order" is discussed in detail in Don Oberdorfer, "Bush's Talk of a 'New World Order': Foreign Policy Tool or Mere Slogan?" *Washington Post*, August 26, 1991, pp. A31, A36.

8. Michael Mandelbaum, quoted in Bill Javetski and others, "Winning the Peace: A Stable Mideast Will Be Harder to Achieve Than Military Victory," *Business Week*, March 11, 1991, p. 25; see also Peter W. Rodman, "Middle East Diplomacy after the Gulf War," *Foreign Affairs*, vol. 70 (Spring 1991), pp. 1–18.

9. Jim Hoagland, "The New Gulf Leader," *Washington Post*, February 28, 1991, p. A19.

10. These policy initiatives emerged from an interagency commission, chaired by Deputy National Security Adviser Robert Gates, that was convened after the air war against Iraq opened. The conclusions of the commission were presented before Congress on February 6 and 7, 1991, by Secretary of State Baker. See "Waging the Peace," *Middle East Policy Survey*, no. 64 (February 1, 1991); and Carroll J. Doherty, "U.S. May Have to Start from Scratch in the

Volatile Postwar Arab World," *Congressional Quarterly*, February 23, 1991, pp. 472–73.

11. Ann Devroy, "President Proposes Mideast Arms Curb," *Washington Post*, May 30, 1991, pp. A1, A35; and Andrew Rosenthal, "Bush Unveils Plan for Arms Control in the Middle East," *New York Times*, May 30, 1991, pp. A1, A19.

12. David Hoffman, "Shamir Plan Was to Stall Autonomy," *Washington Post*, June 27, 1992, p. A13.

13. See, for example, the remarks of a senior American official shepherding the multilateral talks, in "Dennis Ross Says Arms Control Tops U.S. Middle East Policy," *al-Fajr*, August 10, 1992, p. 15.

14. The first round of multilateral talks was held in Moscow in January 1992; see Gerald Butt, "The Moscow Talks: Flagging Arab Spirits," *Middle East International*, February 7, 1992, pp. 4–5; and Magda Abu Fadil and Drew Harrison, "That Was Not the Idea," *The Middle East*, no. 209 (March 1992), pp. 21–23. In May 1992 a session of the multilateral talks devoted entirely to arms control convened in Washington; see R. Jeffrey Smith, "State Department Meeting on Mideast Arms Control Opens without Rancor," *Washington Post*, May 12, 1992, p. A12; and John M. Goshko, "Israeli-Arab Arms Control Talks End Here," *Washington Post*, May 15, 1992, p. A26. For the Syrian and Lebanese boycott, see Salwa Ustuwani, "Syrian Information Minister Tells *al-Sharq al-Awsat*: We Reaffirm Our Confidence in U.S. Administration and Refuse to Participate in Multilateral Negotiations until Israeli Position Changes," *al-Sharq al-Awsat*, May 13, 1992, in Foreign Broadcast Information Service, *Daily Report: Near East and South Asia*, May 14, 1992, p. 32; Tony Walker, "Arabs May Boycott Moscow Peace Talks," *Financial Times*, January 20, 1992, p. 4; and Sameh Abdullah, "Timing the Multilateral Talks," *al-Ahram Weekly*, January 23, 1992, p. 3.

15. Lee Feinstein, "U.S. Arms Transfers to Middle East Dampen Prospects for Paris Meeting," *Arms Control Today*, vol. 21 (July–August 1991), pp. 23, 31; J. A. C. Lewis, "UN Five Agree to Curb Exports," *Jane's Defence Weekly*, July 20, 1991, p. 86; Lee Feinstein, "'Big Five' Weapons Exporters: More Talks, More Sales," *Arms Control Today*, vol. 21 (November 1991), pp. 15, 22–23; "Washington Arms Trade Meeting Shows Scant Results," *Basic Reports*, no. 22 (June 3, 1992), pp. 1–2; Elaine Sciolino, "Arms Vendors Fail to Impose Limits," *New York Times*, May 31, 1992, p. A12; and Lee Feinstein, "Third Round of Arms Sales Talks Fails to Resolve Notification Issue," *Arms Control Today*, vol. 22 (June 1992), p. 21.

16. Amos Perlmutter, "Arms Control for the Middle East?" *Washington Times*, May 23, 1991, p. G1.

17. David Silverberg, "U.S. Sees Need for Mideast Arms Control in Gulf War's Wake," *Defense News*, May 6, 1991, p. 16.

18. Geoffrey Kemp, "The Middle East Arms Race: Can It Be Controlled?" *Middle East Journal*, vol. 45 (Summer 1991), p. 455.

19. The current borders in the Middle East, like those in the third world generally, were imposed largely by the European powers after World War I;

see E. R. Leach, "The Frontiers of 'Burma,'" *Comparative Studies in Society and History*, vol. 3 (1960), pp. 49–68; and David Fromkin, *A Peace to End All Peace: The Fall of the Ottoman Empire and the Creation of the Modern Middle East* (Avon Books, 1989). This border-inventing process continues today: witness the Western role in redefining the Iraqi-Kuwaiti border after the Gulf War. See Tony Horwitz, "Is This Kuwait? No, This is Iraq. Really? Well, Not Exactly," *Wall Street Journal*, December 5, 1991, pp. A1, A6; G. H. Jansen, "The Iraq-Kuwait Boundary: The Umm Qasr Time Bomb," *Middle East International*, March 6, 1992, pp. 8–9; and Caryle Murphy, "U.N. Map Makers Draw Kuwaiti-Iraqi Border," *Washington Post*, May 5, 1992, pp. A19, A20. Other currently contested borders in the region include those between Morocco and the Sahrawi Republic, and Libya and Chad; all the borders surrounding mandate Palestine; the Iskenderun district between Syria and Turkey; long, marshy stretches between Iran and Iraq; and all the obscure desert tracks dividing the emirates of Arabia.

20. On the primacy of politics as a motor of regional arms races, see Yezid Sayigh, "Arab Regional Security: Between Mechanics and Politics," *RUSI Journal*, vol. 136 (Summer 1991), pp. 38–46.

21. Marvin Feuerwerger, *The Arrow Next Time? Israel's Missile Defense Program for the 1990s* (Washington: Washington Institute for Near East Policy, 1991), p. 2.

22. Thomas L. McNaugher, "Ballistic Missiles and Chemical Weapons: The Legacy of the Iran-Iraq War," *International Security*, vol. 15 (Fall 1990), p. 9. Ironically, the Chinese and North Koreans acquired their first Scud-Bs from the Egyptians.

23. W. Andrew Terrill, "The Gulf War and Ballistic Missile Proliferation," *Comparative Strategy*, vol. 11 (1992), pp. 163–76.

24. Janne E. Nolan and Albert D. Wheelon, "Third World Ballistic Missiles," *Scientific American*, vol. 263 (August 1990), p. 36; and John R. Harvey and Uzi Rubin, "Controlling Ballistic Missiles: How Important? How to Do It?" *Arms Control Today*, vol. 22 (March 1992), p. 15.

25. Aaron Karp, *The United States and the Soviet Union and the Control of Ballistic Missile Proliferation to the Middle East* (New York: Institute for East-West Security Studies, 1990), p. 28.

26. John W. Lewis, Hua Di, and Xue Litai, "Beijing's Defense Establishment," *International Security*, vol. 15 (Spring 1991), p. 107.

27. See Nadev Safran, *Israel: The Embattled Ally* (Harvard University Press, Belknap Press, 1978), p. 239; and Ze'ev Schiff, *A History of the Israeli Army: 1874 to the Present* (Macmillan, 1985), pp. 115–23.

28. The argument about the inapplicability of Western-style arms control measures to the Middle East is made very forcefully in Geoffrey Kemp, with the assistance of Shelley A. Stahl, *The Control of the Middle East Arms Race* (Washington: Carnegie Endowment for International Peace, 1991), pp. 15–46.

29. According to Goldring, *Arms Transfers to the Middle East*, table 1, p. 14, between 1984 and 1988, 29.9 percent of all arms imported by the Middle East came from the Soviet Union, 18.3 percent from the United States, 14.3

percent from France, 9.3 percent from China, and 3.5 percent from the United Kingdom.

30. For these diverse factors, see Andrew J. Pierre, *The Global Politics of Arms Sales* (Princeton University Press, 1982); and Michael T. Klare, *American Arms Supermarket* (University of Texas Press, 1984). Recent studies suggest that if the United States restricted its arms sales to the Middle East to $700 million per country, it would be able to reduce its defense budget by $10 billion per year—even though it would lose $3 billion a year in exports; see "Restrict Arms and Save Money Says Congress," *Middle East Economic Digest*, October 9, 1992, p. 6.

31. *World Oil Trends*, 1991 ed. (Cambridge, Mass.: Arthur Andersen & Co., S.C., and Cambridge Energy Associates, 1991), p. 39.

32. Daniel P. Hewitt, "Military Expenditures in the Developing World," *Finance and Development*, vol. 28 (September 1991), table 1, p. 23, and table 2, p. 25.

33. This argument is epitomized by David Pryce-Jones, *The Closed Circle: An Interpretation of the Arabs* (Harper and Row, 1989). Unfortunately, there are few serious studies that analyze the patterns of violence in the Middle East. The most noteworthy exception is Şerif Mardin, "Youth and Violence in Turkey," *European Journal of Sociology*, vol. 19 (1978), pp. 229–54.

34. One of the few studies to make serious mention of the role of economic forces in this context is Alan Platt, ed., *Report of the Study Group on Multilateral Arms Transfer Guidelines for the Middle East* (Washington: Henry L. Stimson Center, May 1992).

CHAPTER 2

1. This chapter draws on my essay, "Economic Crisis in the Arab World: Catalyst for Conflict," *Policy Focus* (Overseas Development Council), no. 5 (September 1991).

2. International Monetary Fund, *International Financial Statistics Yearbook, 1991* (Washington, 1991), pp. 460–63. Unless otherwise specified, all currency values are quoted in current (rather than constant) terms.

3. "Arab Aid Reaches a Turning Point," *Middle East Economic Digest*, December 21, 1990, p. 6. (Hereafter *MEED*.)

4. UN Development Programme (UNDP), *Human Development Report, 1992* (Oxford University Press, 1992), pp. 170–71.

5. UNDP, *Human Development Report, 1992*, pp. 152–53; *FAO Trade Yearbook, 1986*, series 96, vol. 40 (Rome: Food and Agriculture Organization [FAO] of the United Nations, 1987), pp. 311–74; and *FAO Yearbook: Trade, 1989*, series 96, vol. 43 (Rome: FAO, 1990), pp. 317–80.

6. Saleh S. Jallad, "Arab Economies until 1993," *MEED*, March 24, 1989, p. 14; Sadowski, "Economic Crisis in the Arab World," p. 7; and World Bank, *World Debt Tables, 1991–92: External Debt of Developing Countries*, vol. 2:

Country Tables (Washington: World Bank, 1991), p. xxiii. For an even more dramatic set of figures, see Andrew Cunningham, "Leaving Debtors Out in the Cold," *MEED*, January 12, 1990, pp. 4–5.

7. The most precise calculations of Iraq's war damages are by Kamran Mofid, who thinks they totaled $452.6 billion. Mofid, *The Economic Consequences of the Gulf War* (New York: Routledge, 1990), p. 133. See also Anthony H. Cordesman, *The Iran-Iraq War and Western Security, 1984–87: Strategic Implications and Policy Options* (London: Jane's, 1987), p. 9; and Marion Farouk-Sluglett and Peter Sluglett, "Iraq since 1986: The Strengthening of Saddam," *Middle East Report*, vol. 20 (November–December 1990), p. 20.

8. Elaine Sciolino, *The Outlaw State: Saddam Hussein's Quest for Power and the Gulf Crisis* (John Wiley and Sons, 1991), pp. 183–204.

9. Steven Mufson, "Iraq's Ability to Pay Reparations Doubted," *Washington Post*, March 1, 1991, p. A29; and Efraim Karsh and Inari Rautsi, *Saddam Hussein: A Political Biography* (Free Press, 1991), pp. 194–216.

10. Sharif Ghalib, "Iraq: Debt, Imports, Food Stocks," Institute of International Finance, Inc., Washington, August 14, 1990. See also "Iraq: Baghdad Reveals Debt Obligations," *MEED*, May 24, 1991, p. 19; Jonathan Crusoe, "Iraq: Still Living on Credit," *MEED*, November 25, 1988; pp. 4–5; and World Bank, *World Debt Tables, 1991–92*, vol. 2: *Country Tables*.

11. Adel Darwish and Gregory Alexander, *Unholy Babylon: The Secret History of Saddam's War* (St. Martin's Press, 1991), pp. 228–78.

12. Tom Kono, "The Economics behind the Invasion," *Middle East Insight*, vol. 7 (December 1990), pp. 36–41; Edmund O'Sullivan, "OPEC: Getting That Sinking Feeling," *MEED*, July 13, 1990, pp. 4–5; and Youssef M. Ibrahim, "Threat Issued by Iraqis on Oil Overproduction," *New York Times*, July 18, 1990, pp. D1, D5.

13. Caryle Murphy, "Iraqi Leader Gets New Title as Kuwaiti Anxiety Grows," *Washington Post*, July 20, 1990, p. A12.

14. Barton Gellman, "U.S. Bombs Missed 70% of Time," *Washington Post*, March 16, 1991, pp. A1, A18. See also Paul F. Walker and Eric Stambler, ". . . And the Dirty Little Weapons," *Bulletin of the Atomic Scientists*, vol. 47 (May 1991), pp. 20–24; and Barton Gellman, "Gulf Weapons' Accuracy Downgraded," *Washington Post*, April 10, 1992, pp. A1, A37.

15. Barton Gellman, "Allied Air War Struck Broadly in Iraq," *Washington Post*, June 23, 1991, p. A1.

16. Gellman, "Allied Air War Struck Broadly in Iraq," p. A16; Jonathan Crusoe, "Iraq: The Electricity Gap," *MEED*, August 30, 1991, p. 8; James Placke, "Oil Sector Recovery in Kuwait and Iraq: How Long, How Difficult," Decision Brief, Cambridge Energy Research Associates, April 1991, p. 4; Paul Lewis, "After the War, For Iraqis, a Slow Return to Normality," *New York Times*, May 2, 1991, p. A16; Patrick E. Tyler, "U.S. Officials Believe Iraq Will Take Years to Rebuild," *New York Times*, June 3, 1991, p. A8; and Iraqi Housing and Construction Minister Mahmoud Dhiyab al-Ahmed, quoted in Alan Cowell, "Baghdad Rebuilds but Has Far to Go," *New York Times*, June 11, 1991, p. A10.

17. *Report to the Secretary-General on Humanitarian Needs in Kuwait and Iraq in the Immediate Post-Crisis Environment by a Mission to the Area Led by Mr. Martti Ahtisaari, Under-Secretary-General for Administration and Management, dated 20 March 1991*, UN Document S/22366 (UN Security Council, March 20, 1991), p. 5.

18. Tyler, "U.S. Officials Believe Iraq Will Take Years to Rebuild."

19. "Iraq: Baghdad Reveals Debt Obligations," p. 19. Interpreting these figures, which were submitted by Iraq to the United Nations, is tricky. In addition to its budget for reconstruction, Iraq also projected spending $93 billion over five years on "development projects." Much of this "development" spending is probably for reconstruction.

20. Trevor Rowe, "U.N. Studying War-Damage Assessment," *Washington Post*, May 15, 1991, p. A24; Edmund O'Sullivan, "The UN Calls Iraq to Account," *MEED*, May 17, 1991, p. 7; and George Lardner, Jr., "U.S. Intelligence Reports Signs Iran is Getting Food to Iraq," *Washington Post*, September 25, 1990, p. A18.

21. William Arkin, quoted in Simon Edge, "Iraq: Turning Humiliation on Its Head," *MEED*, January 24, 1992, p. 14. The Iraqi civil war, particularly the insurrection by Shi'i dissidents who tried desperately to overthrow Saddam's regime in March 1991, caused the majority of these civilian deaths. See William M. Arkin, Damian Durrant, and Marianne Cherni, "On Impact: Modern Warfare and the Environment: A Case Study of the Gulf War," Study prepared for a "Fifth Geneva" Convention on the Protection of the Environment in Time of Armed Conflict, 3 June 1991, London, UK (Washington: Greenpeace, May 1991), p. 15.

22. Bill Frelick, *Mass Exodus: Iraqi Refugees in Iran* (Washington: U.S. Committee for Refugees, May 1991).

23. Peter Fuhrman, "Robbin' Hood," *Forbes*, March 18, 1991, p. 43.

24. "Iraq: Severe Food Shortages Anticipated," *MEED*, March 22, 1991, pp. 12–13; and Alan Cowell, "Sanctions on Iraq Exact a High Price from Poor," *New York Times*, June 9, 1991, p. 14.

25. "Iraq: Living on Less," *MEED*, June 21, 1991, p. 7; and Mark Nicholson, "Iraqi Food Prices 'Climb by 1,500%,'" *Financial Times*, October 23, 1991, p. 4.

26. Tony Horwitz, "In Iraq Today, Children Scavenge for Food, Economists Drive Cabs," *Wall Street Journal*, July 15, 1991, p. A8.

27. Dr. Harvey V. Fineberg, Dean, Harvard School of Public Health, quoted in Patrick E. Tyler, "Health Crisis Said to Grip Iraq in Wake of War's Destruction," *New York Times*, May 22, 1991, p. 16.

28. Nicholson, "Iraqi Food Prices 'Climb by 1,500%.'"

29. "The Great Hunger," *The Economist*, July 20, 1991, pp. 42–43.

30. David Powell, "Iraq: Appeal against Sanctions," *Middle East International*, November 8, 1991, p. 13.

31. Powell, "Iraq: Appeal against Sanctions," pp. 13–14; "Iraq: Infrastructure Nears Breakdown," *MEED*, November 1, 1991, pp. 13–14; David Brown, "Study Says Iraqi Children Dying at Accelerated Rate," *Washington Post*, Oc-

tober 23, 1991, p. A3; and Pat Lancaster, "Iraq: The Aftermath," *The Middle East*, no. 206 (December 1991), pp. 45–48. For an excellent overview, see Jean Dreze and Haris Gazdar, "Hunger and Poverty in Iraq, 1991," *World Development*, vol. 20 (1992), pp. 921–45.

32. "Heads You Win, Tails I Lose," *The Economist*, September 1, 1990, pp. 38–39; Hugh Carnegy and Lamis Andoni, "Jordan Sees Economic Disaster," *Financial Times*, September 3, 1990, p. 2; and Sirin Halasah, *Jordan Times*, September 12, 1990, p. 3, in Foreign Broadcast Information Service, *Daily Report: Near East and South Asia*, September 12, 1990, pp. 42–43. (Hereafter FBIS, *Near East*.)

33. "Minister Details Country's Economic Situation," *al-Ra'y*, September 20, 1990, p. 10, in FBIS, *Near East*, September 20, 1990, pp. 33–36. GNP figures are from "Jordan: Economy Shrinks by 17 Per Cent," *MEED*, September 20, 1991, p. 15.

34. Arkin, Durrant, and Cherni, "Modern Warfare and the Environment," p. 15.

35. Youssef M. Ibrahim, "Saudi Curbs on Yemeni Workers Set Off a Migration," *New York Times*, October 22, 1990, p. A10; Judith Miller, "Yemen's Chief Assails Saudis on Gulf Crisis," *New York Times*, October 26, 1990, pp. A1, A11; David Pike, "Saudi Arabia Retaliates for Lack of Support," *MEED*, October 5, 1990, p. 22; and Nora Boustany, "Jordan, Saudis Feud over Truck Traffic," *Washington Post*, October 2, 1990, p. A16.

36. Shaikh Jaber al-Ahmed al-Sabah, Emir of Kuwait, quoted in "A Victory Turned Sour: Human Rights in Kuwait since Liberation," *Middle East Watch Report* (New York and Washington: Human Rights Watch, September 1991), p. 5; "Asian Expatriates: Coming Back," *The Middle East*, no. 204 (October 1991), p. 36; Simon Edge, "Migrants Come Home to Roost," *MEED*, October 4, 1991, pp. 4–6; and "Kuwait Looks Eastward," *The Economist*, November 30, 1991, p. 41.

37. Youssef M. Ibrahim, "For Refugees in Jordan, Misery without End," *New York Times*, October 3, 1991, pp. A1, A10; "Jordan: Resettling Returnees to Cost $4.5 Billion," *MEED*, September 20, 1991, p. 15; "Minister Details Country's Economic Situation"; Jackson Diehl, "Gulf War Migrants Add to Jordan's Woes," *Washington Post*, February 19, 1992, pp. A21, A22; and "Jordan: Economy Shrinks by 17 Per Cent," p. 15.

38. Ministry of Planning, Jordan, "The Financial Burden of the Jordanian Returnees on the Economy (Preliminary Report)," September 7, 1991, p. 2. These figures are slightly higher than the estimates of the UN Economic and Social Commission for West Asia; see "Jordan," *MEED*, November 8, 1991, p. 17.

39. For a detailed study of the combined effects of these changes, see Jawda 'Abd al-Khaliq, *al-In'ikasat al-Iqtisadiyya lil-Ghazw al-'Iraqi lil-Kuwayt min al-Manzur al-Istratiji* (Economic effects of the Iraqi invasion of Kuwait from a strategic vantage point) (Cairo: Markaz al-Buhuth wal-Dirasat al-Iqtisadiyya wal-Maliyya, January 1991).

40. Edmund O'Sullivan, "Making Iraq Pay for Its War," *MEED*, May 31, 1991, pp. 4–5.

41. International Monetary Fund, *World Economic Outlook, October 1991* (Washington, 1991), p. 22.

42. "1500 Milyar Dular Qimat Khasa'ir Harb al-Khalij fil-Kuwait wal-Iraq" ($1500 billion is the price of the losses of the Gulf War in Kuwait and Iraq), *al-Shira'*, May 18, 1992, p. 12. See also Mishal Bunajm, "I'timad Amirka 'ala al-Naft al-'Arabi Sayuzdadu wa-Mintaqat al-Khalij Khasarat Ba'd Harbayn 800 Milyar Dular" (The dependence of America on Arab oil will increase and the Gulf region lost $800 billion as a result of its two wars), *al-Wasat*, May 11, 1992, pp. 37–39.

43. Ibrahim M. Oweiss, "Economic Impact of the Gulf War with Special Reference to the Economies of Selected Arab Countries," Georgetown University, Department of Economics, April 19, 1991, p. 8; Anthony H. Cordesman, "No End of a Lesson? Iraq and the Issue of Arms Transfers," *RUSI Journal*, vol. 136 (Spring 1991), p. 3; Youssef M. Ibrahim, "Gulf War's Cost to Arabs Estimated at $620 Billion," *New York Times*, September 8, 1992, p. A4; and "Khasa'ir al-'Arab min Ghazu al-Kuwayt 620 Milyar Dular" (The losses of the Arabs from the invasion of Kuwait are $620 billion), *al-Majalla*, October 14–20, 1992, p. 64.

44. The town of al-Khafji, near the Kuwaiti border, was devastated, but the cost of physical reconstruction here is minor. See Mahir 'Abbas, "al-Khafji: Tawat Safhat al-Azma wa-Ra'a Ahluha al-Shams" (al-Khafji: Done with the crisis and its people see the sun), *al-Majalla*, November 20–26, 1991, pp. 7–11.

45. "Saudi Arabia: Deposit Flight Reached $4.4 Billion in August," *MEED*, October 19, 1990, p. 36; Victor Mallet, "Crisis in the Gulf: Saudi Industry Watches Investors' Confidence Drain Away," *Financial Times*, August 21, 1990, p. 3; and "Saudi Arabia: Gulf Crisis Triggers Exodus of Private Savings," *MEED*, September 21, 1990, pp. 26–27.

46. David B. Ottaway, "Saudi Puts Crisis Costs in Billions," *Washington Post*, August 21, 1990, p. A8; and "Saudi Arabia: Gulf Crisis to Cost Billions of Dollars," *MEED*, August 31, 1990, pp. 18–19. See also Michael Field, "Exiles Await 'Day of Return,'" *Financial Times*, December 12, 1990, p. III.

47. "Saudi Arabia: UK to Get Cash for War Costs," *MEED*, May 3, 1991, p. 21.

48. David B. Ottaway, "Saudis, Said to Owe $64 Billion, Scrape to Meet Obligations," *Washington Post*, April 3, 1991, pp. A25, A26.

49. Lara Marlowe, "US Takes Initiative in a Revitalised Market," *Financial Times*, December 12, 1990, p. II; and "The Arab World's Arms Shopping List," *Jerusalem Report*, August 1, 1991, p. 17.

50. Thomas W. Lippman, "Saudis to Accelerate Oil Production Plans," *Washington Post*, October 12, 1990, pp. F1, F4; Youssef M. Ibrahim, "Saudi Oil Exports Rise to New High, Easing Shortage," *New York Times*, November 4, 1990, pp. 1, 16; and "Saudi Arabia: Gulf Crisis Will Cost $21 Billion in 1990," *MEED*, December 14, 1990, p. 19.

51. Judith Miller, "Saudis Importing Fuel to Fight War," *New York Times*, January 23, 1991, p. 6.

52. "Saudi Arabia: Gulf Crisis Will Cost $21 Billion in 1990," p. 19. See also David Pike, "MEED Special Report: Saudi Arabia," *MEED*, November 8, 1991, p. VI; and "Saudi Arabia: Crisis Spending Details Emerge," *MEED*, January 18, 1991, p. 18.

53. Andrew Cunningham, "Saudi Arabia: Why the Kingdom Has to Borrow," *The Middle East*, no. 207 (January 1992), p. 35.

54. See Mark Nicholson, "Gulf Crisis Forces Saudi Arabia to Delay Budget," *Financial Times*, January 2, 1991, p. 3.

55. Ron Cooper, "The Enigma behind the Saudi Billions," *Euromoney*, September 1990, p. 75.

56. "Gulf States Give US More War Cash," *MEED*, August 23, 1991, p. 7.

57. "Saudi Arabia: Saudi Aramco to Raise $1.5 Billion Loan," *MEED*, October 4, 1991, p. 36; "Saudi Arabia: Can You Spare a Few Billion?" *The Middle East*, no. 202 (August 1991), p. 35; Stanley Reed, "Cash Squeeze? What Cash Squeeze?" *Business Week*, May 13, 1991, p. 58; and Edmund O'Sullivan, "Gulf States Test the Banks," *MEED*, July 19, 1991, pp. 4–5.

58. David Pike, "The Resilience of Saudi Arabia," *MEED*, May 24, 1991, p. 4.

59. "Kuwait: Hands on the Till," *The Middle East*, no. 204 (October 1991), pp. 32–33; "Digging Deep to Find Money for the War," *MEED*, February 8, 1991, p. 6; Craig Forman, "Kuwait's Broken Economy Resists Repair," *Wall Street Journal*, May 30, 1991, p. A11; Jonathan Crusoe, "MEED Special Report: Kuwait," *MEED*, January 17, 1992, pp. III–VIII; and Jonathan Crusoe, "The Test Continues for Kuwait," *MEED*, August 9, 1991, pp. 4–5.

60. For the Gulf states' policy of punishing Arab countries that did not join the alliance, see Wahib Gharab, "Muwajahat al-Nizam al-'Iraqi wal-Muta'winin Ma'ahu" (Confronting the Iraqi regime and those who cooperated with it), *al-Majalla*, January 1–7, 1992, p. 20.

61. Hisham Milhim, "'Displeasure' with Kuwait," Paris Radio Monte Carlo, May 10, 1991, in FBIS, *Near East*, May 10, 1991, pp. 3–4; Caryle Murphy, "Egypt's Pullout Signals Discord with Gulf," *Washington Post*, May 11, 1991, p. A18; Max Rodenbeck, "Why Mubarak did a U-turn on the Gulf," *Middle East International*, May 17, 1991, p. 3; and Jalal Duwaydar, "A Position Expressing Disappointment," *al-Akhbar*, September 27, 1991, p. 1, in FBIS, *Near East*, October 3, 1991, pp. 5–6.

62. The consensus among petroleum analysts has been that in the first half of the 1990s oil prices will run only barely ahead of the rate of inflation. Experts also hope that by the late 1990s global oil demand may begin to exceed supply and OPEC producers may once again enjoy real increases in prices. See Geoffrey Heal and Graciela Chichilnisky, *Oil and the International Economy* (Oxford: Clarendon Press, 1991), p. 70; and Wilfred L. Kohl, ed., *After the Oil Price Collapse* (Johns Hopkins University Press, 1991), pp. 200–01.

63. Hugh Carnegy and Tony Walker, "De Facto Disarmament," *Financial Times*, September 4, 1989, p. 19.

64. Robert Pear, "Arms Sales to Third World Said to Decline Sharply," *New York Times*, June 21, 1990, p. A10. This sort of trend is not without precedent in the Arab world. After the October 1973 war, Egypt faced a major economic crisis and responded by making steady cuts in its military expenditures for five years. This trend ended only after Cairo signed the Camp David accords—for which the United States rewarded it with lavish military aid. See Stephen Green and Frank Bonvillain, "Egypt's Unilateral Disarmament: A Failed Experiment," *American-Arab Affairs*, no. 12 (Spring 1985), pp. 50–58.

65. Eric J. Hobsbawm, *The Age of Empire, 1875–1914* (Vintage Books, 1987), p. 62.

CHAPTER 3

1. "Election Watch," *Journal of Democracy*, vol. 3 (April 1992), p. 122.

2. For a perceptive analysis of this issue, see Jim Coffman, "Choosing the Veil," *Mother Jones*, November–December 1991, pp. 23–24.

3. Jonathan C. Randal, "Algerian Leader Quits, Imperiling Power Shift to Muslims," *Washington Post*, January 12, 1992, p. A23; and Jonathan C. Randal, "Algerian Elections Cancelled," *Washington Post*, January 13, 1992, p. A1.

4. U.S. Arms Control and Disarmament Agency (ACDA), *World Military Expenditures and Arms Transfers, 1985*, ACDA publication no. 123 (1985), pp. 49, 59, 66, 67, 91, 101, 108, 109; and UN Development Programme, *Human Development Report, 1991* (Oxford University Press, 1991), pp. 156–57.

5. The human development index (HDI) is an aggregate measure of development reflecting (1) per capita income adjusted to remove exchange rate distortions; (2) average level of education and literacy; and (3) life expectancy. See *Human Development Report, 1991*.

6. World Bank, *World Development Report, 1991* (Oxford University Press, 1991), pp. 214–15.

7. *World Development Report, 1991*, pp. 222, 223; and World Bank, *World Development Report, 1988* (Oxford University Press, 1988), pp. 204, 205.

8. For a sophisticated analysis of the obstacles to development in the Arab world, see Alan Richards and John Waterbury, *A Political Economy of the Middle East* (Boulder, Colo.: Westview Press, 1990). For a detailed case study, see Yahya M. Sadowski, *Political Vegetables? Businessman and Bureaucrat in the Development of Egyptian Agriculture* (Brookings, 1991).

9. For examples of such reasoning, see Gamal Zayida, "Sira' al-Silah wal-Tanmiyya fi al-Sharq al-Awsat" (The conflict of arms and development in the Middle East), *al-Ahram al-Iqtisadi*, January 28, 1991, p. 25; and Rafaat Soliman, "Slow Rate of Arab Social Development," *al-Ahram Weekly*, January 9, 1991, p. 4.

10. This case has been made with particular force by Robert Looney; see his "Defense Expenditures and Human Capital Development in the Middle East and South Asia," *International Journal of Social Economics*, vol. 17 (1990), pp. 4–16; and "Guns versus Butter in the Middle East: Paradoxes Surrounding the Economic Impact of Defense Expenditures," *Japanese Institute of Middle Eastern Economies Review*, no. 15 (Winter 1992), pp. 57–73. For more critical assessments of the economic impact of military expenditures, see Nicole Ball, *Security and Economy in the Third World* (Princeton University Press, 1988); and Saadet Deger, *Military Expenditure in Third World Countries* (London: Routledge and Kegan Paul, 1986).

11. Janne E. Nolan, *Military Industry in Taiwan and South Korea* (Macmilllan, 1986). For an overview of Arab military industrialization efforts, see Yezid Sayigh, *Arab Military Industry: Capability, Performance and Impact* (London: Brassey's, 1992).

12. For the politics of military industrialization in Egypt, see Robert Springborg, "The President and the Field Marshall: Civil-Military Relations in Egypt Today," *Middle East Report*, vol. 17 (July–August 1987), pp. 4–16; and Ahmad Abdallah, ed., *al-Jaysh wal-Dimuqratiyya fi Misr* (The army and democracy in Egypt) (Cairo: Sina' lil-Nashr, 1990). For arms industries in the Arab world generally, see Andrew L. Ross, "Do-It-Yourself Weaponry," *Bulletin of the Atomic Scientists*, vol. 46 (May 1990), pp. 20–22; and Yazid Sayegh, "The Changing Fortunes of the Arab Military Industry," *al-Ahram Weekly*, May 6, 1992, p. 5. For a dissenting voice, see Robert E. Looney, "The Impact of Defence Expenditures on Arab Industrial Development," *Arms Control*, vol. 12 (September 1991), pp. 304–24.

13. Michael C. Dunn, "Egypt: From Domestic Needs to Export Market," in James Everett Katz, ed., *The Implications of Third World Military Industrialization* (Lexington Books, 1986), pp. 119–34; Michael C. Dunn, "Arming for Peacetime: Egypt's Defense Industry Today," *Defense and Foreign Affairs*, October–November 1988; and Philip Finnegan, "Egyptian Arms Makers Shift to Civil Goods," *Defense News*, March 16, 1992, p. 12. For the stagnation of military industrialization programs in the Arab world, see Geoffrey Kemp, *The Control of the Middle East Arms Race* (Washington: Carnegie Endowment for International Peace, 1991), pp. 86–88. As a policy issue, military industrialization in the Arab world is not seen as a threat; see Office of Technology Assessment, U.S. Congress, *Global Arms Trade: Commerce in Advanced Military Technology and Weapons*, OTA-ISC-460 (Government Printing Office, June 1991).

14. Steve Coll, "New Saudi Arms Business Still Enriches Old Elite," *Washington Post*, October 8, 1990, p. A1; and "Kuwait: Defence Ministry Changes Agency Rules," *Middle East Economic Digest*, March 6, 1992, p. 17 (hereafter *MEED*).

15. When Arabs are not ruled by officers, they are often ruled by monarchs, such as King Hussein of Jordan and Sultan Qabus of Oman, whose military education (Sandhurst) and style of rule functionally make them members of the officer corps.

16. The best analyses of military coups in the Arab world are Eliezer Beeri, "The Waning of the Military Coup in Arab Politics," *Middle Eastern Studies*, vol. 18 (January 1982), pp. 69–81; and Hanna Batatu, *The Egyptian, Syrian and Iraqi Revolutions: Some Observations on Their Underlying Causes and Social Character* (Georgetown University Center for Contemporary Arabic Studies, 1983). See also Gabriel Ben-Dor, "Civilianization of Military Regimes in the Arab World," in Henry Bienen and David Morell, eds., *Political Participation under Military Regimes* (Sage, 1976), pp. 39–49.

17. For an excellent discussion of this, see Yezid Sayigh, "Confronting the 1990s: Security in the Developing Countries," *Adelphi Papers*, no. 251 (Summer 1990).

18. UN Development Programme, *Human Development Report, 1990* (Oxford University Press, 1990), pp. 150–51; and Sadowski, *Political Vegetables?* p. 17.

19. E. A. Wayne, "Aoun Wins Praise from Some Muslim Leaders," *Christian Science Monitor*, April 7, 1989, p. 6; Richard Donkin, "Network of Companies with Baghdad Ties," *Financial Times*, September 21, 1989, p. 6; and Giles Trendle, "Lebanon: Time to Clean Up the Act," *The Middle East*, no. 205 (November 1991), p. 20.

20. Sadiq Jalal al-'Azm, *al-Naqd al-Dhati Ba'd al-Hazima* (Self-criticism after the disaster) (Beirut: Dar al-Tali'a, 1969).

21. U.S. News and World Report, *Triumph without Victory: The Unreported History of the Persian Gulf War* (Times Books, 1992), pp. 403–6.

22. The only "bright spots" for the Arabs were the performance of a few Saudi jet fighters (working with American air targeting controllers) and a Qatari tank brigade. For an excellent assessment of the political and technical constraints on the battlefield performance of Arab troops during the Gulf War, see Deborah Amos, *Lines in the Sand* (Simon and Schuster, 1992).

23. Ehud Ya'ari, "A Slap in Egypt's Face," *Jerusalem Report*, June 6, 1991, p. 5.

24. David B. Ottaway, "For Saudi Military, New Self-Confidence," *Washington Post*, April 20, 1991, p. A12.

25. The rapidly changing thinking of Arab officers about the implications of the Gulf War can be traced in journals such as *al-Difa' al-'Arabi* and *Istratijiyya*.

26. For a discussion of the new battlefield technologies, see William J. Perry, "Desert Storm and Deterrence," *Foreign Affairs*, vol. 70 (Fall 1990), pp. 66–82.

27. For Israel's high-technology conventional warfare capabilities, see W. Seth Carus and Hirsh Goodman, *The Future Battlefield and the Arab-Israeli Conflict* (New Brunswick, N.J.: Transaction Publishers, 1990).

28. See Gordon Richards, "Stabilization Crises and the Breakdown of Military Authoritarianism in Latin America," *Comparative Political Studies*, vol. 18 (January 1986), pp. 449–85; and Karen L. Remmer, "Democracy and Economic Crisis: The Latin American Experience," *World Politics*, vol. 42 (April 1990), pp. 315–35.

29. In Jordan, Algeria, and, to a lesser extent, Egypt, the government responded to economic crisis by offering moves toward democratization. But the political liberalization in these countries offers the public limited compensation for economic hardship, not a promise of a real change of regime. See Michael C. Hudson, "The Possibilities for Pluralism," *American-Arab Affairs*, no. 36 (Spring 1991), pp. 3–5.

30. For the bonds among Arab officers, see Eliezer Beeri, *Army Officers in Arab Politics and Society* (Praeger, 1970); Alasdair Drysdale, "The Syrian Armed Forces in National Politics: The Role of the Geographic and Ethnic Periphery," in Roman Kolkowicz and Andrezj Korbonski, eds., *Soldiers, Peasants and Bureaucrats* (London: George Allen and Unwin, 1982), pp. 52–76; and Ghassane Salameh, "Political Power and the Saudi State," *MERIP Reports*, no. 91 (October 1980), pp. 5–23.

31. Western journalists, appalled that the Asad regime was willing to demolish Syria's third largest city to win a civil war, coined the term "Hama rules" to describe the no-holds-barred desperation with which the regime defended its power. (See Thomas L. Friedman, *From Beirut to Jerusalem* [Farrar Straus Giroux, 1989], pp. 76–105.) But "Hama rules" are not a uniquely Syrian phenomenon: they appear wherever the way of life of the military elite is threatened, whether by insurrection or democracy.

32. For an overview of the Syrian economic crisis, see Volker Perthes, "The Syrian Economy in the 1980s," *Middle East Journal*, vol. 46 (Winter 1992), pp. 37–58.

33. Daniel Pipes, "Is Damascus Ready for Peace?" *Foreign Affairs*, vol. 70 (Fall 1991) p. 41.

34. David B. Ottaway, "Israel Uneasy over Word of Syria-Soviet Arms Deal," *Washington Post*, October 25, 1988, p. A21; Ya'aqov Lamdan, *Jerusalem Post*, December 12, 1988, p. 2, in Foreign Broadcast Information Service, *Daily Report: Near East and South Asia*, December 12, 1988, pp. 37–38 (hereafter FBIS, *Near East*); and "USSR to Refurbish Aircraft, Air Defenses," *al-Ittihad*, April 6, 1990, p. 1, in FBIS, *Near East*, April 9, 1990, p. 29.

35. Barbara Opall, "Syria to Buy $2 Billion in Soviet Weapons," *Defense News*, July 8, 1991, p. 3.

36. Ron Ben-Yishay, "al-Asad Is Also Preparing for War," *Yedi'ot Aharanot*, October 29, 1991, in FBIS, *Near East*, October 30, 1991, pp. 35–36; and Meir Rosenne, "Tanks, Planes and Peace Talk," *Jerusalem Post*, November 22, 1991, p. 7.

37. Eric Silver, "Within Striking Distance," *Jerusalem Report*, March 28, 1991, p. 22.

38. *MEED*, November 8, 1991, p. 28; and Joseph S. Bermudez, Jr., "Syria's Acquisition of North Korean 'Scuds,'" *Jane's Intelligence Review*, vol. 3 (June 1991), pp. 249–51.

39. Ben-Yishay, "al-Asad Is Also Preparing for War"; and R. Jeffrey Smith, "U.S. Orders North Korea to Stop Scud Shipment," *Washington Post*, February 22, 1992, p. A15.

40. Mary Battiata, "Czechoslovakia Considers Selling Tanks to Syria, Iran," *Washington Post*, May 7, 1991, p. A25; and Tim Carrington, "Slovak Struggle: Swords to Plowshares," *Wall Street Journal*, October 16, 1991, p. A13.

41. "Military Manpower on the Rise," *MEED*, October 16, 1992, p. 14.

42. Robert Lowry, "Disrupting Czechoslovak Tank Sales to Syria," *al-Ahram Weekly*, February 13, 1992, p. 3.

43. Elaine Sciolino, "U.S. Tracks a Korean Ship Taking Missile to Syria," *New York Times*, February 21, 1991, p. A9; and "al-Asad Yuwajjih 3 Rasa'il ila Amirka wa-Isra'il wa-Du'at 'Tasdir' al-Dimuqratiyya" (al-Asad sends 3 letters to America and Israel and the advocates of "exporting" democracy), *al-Wasat*, March 23, 1992, p. 5.

44. *MEED*, November 8, 1991, p. 28; Ehud Ya'ari, "No M-9s to Syria," *Jerusalem Report*, January 9, 1992, p. 13; and Don Oberdorfer, "China to Reinforce Pledge on Missiles," *Washington Post*, February 2, 1992, p. A17.

45. "In a Friendly Atmosphere," speech delivered by CPSU General Secretary Mikhail Gorbachev at a dinner in honor of Syrian President Hafiz al-Asad, *TASS*, April 25, 1987, in Foreign Broadcast Information Service, *USSR International Affairs*, April 28, 1987, pp. H5–H8. See also Jim Hoagland and Patrick E. Tyler, "Reduced Soviet Arms Flow Weakens Syrian Military," *Washington Post*, September 25, 1987, p. A1; and Tony Walker, "Perestroika's Cooler Winds Reach Syria," *Financial Times*, November 20, 1989, p. 4. For the Syrian reaction to these changes, see Alan Cowell, "Syrian Leader Assails Change in East Bloc as a Boon to Israel," *New York Times*, March 9, 1990, p. A8.

46. Of course, economic pressures for Russia to resume arms exports were gradually building; see Fred Hiatt, "Russia Boosts Weapons Sales to Aid Economy," *Washington Post*, February 23, 1992, p. A1. But Moscow remained less interested in dealing with cash-poor Syria than with countries that could pay hard currency, such as Iran and the Gulf states; see Peter Feuilherade, "Russia and the Gulf: You Can't Beat the Price," *The Middle East*, no. 213 (July 1992), pp. 23–24.

47. Ehud Ya'ari, "A Sad Time for Asad," *Jerusalem Report*, July 4, 1991, p. 36; and On Levi, *Davar*, August 6, 1991, p. 1, in FBIS, *Near East*, August 7, 1991, p. 42.

48. The chief technocrat responsible for pushing liberalization was al-Muhammad 'Imadi, the minister of economy; see "Suriya Tatahawwilu ila Iqtisad al-Suq al-Hurra min khilal al-Qanun Raqm 10" (Syria is becoming a free market economy through law number 10), *al-Majalla*, January 1–7, 1992, pp. 48–49. This trend, in which economic crisis bred increased power for financial technocrats, was apparent around the Arab world. It may have appeared first in Egypt, where it was labeled "the economization of foreign policy"; see Kamal Hasan 'Ali, "al-Bu'd al-Iqtisadi fi Siyasat Misr al-Kharijiyya" (The economic dimension of Egyptian foreign policy), *L'Egypte Contemporaine*, no. 395 (January 1984), pp. 5–25.

49. See "Syria: Investment Law Comes into Force," *MEED*, May 17, 1991, p. 22.

50. "Syria: Gulf War Windfall Boosts Current Account," *MEED*, August 30, 1991, p. 29.

51. Both Saudi Arabia and Kuwait established bilateral economic commissions with Syria after the Iraqi invasion. While these agencies were not interested in delivering cash aid to the Syrian government, they were eager to help raise finance for development projects. See Damascus Domestic Service, April 21, 1991, in FBIS, *Near East*, April 22, 1991, p. 46.

52. "Syria: Budget Attacked by Deputies," *MEED*, May 8, 1992, p. 29.

53. See "Syrie: Besoins de Capitaux" (Syria: Capital needs), *MOCI*, no. 954 (January 7, 1991), pp. 173–74.

54. The quotation is from a Syrian engineer; see Peter Waldman, "Peace Would Pose Risk for Syria's Regime," *Wall Street Journal*, October 29, 1991, p. A18. For similar sentiments, expressed more tactfully, see the open letter to President Asad from 'Umran Adham, a Syrian expatriate businessman, in *al-Hawadeth*, cited in "Syria: Asad Called On to Liberalize Economy and Politics," *MEED*, April 5, 1991, p. 31. See also Nora Boustany, "A Whiff of Peace Stirs the Air in Long-Bellicose Syria," *Washington Post*, July 24, 1992, p. A29.

55. For a description of Syrian fears of Israel, see Patrick Seale, *Asad: The Struggle for the Middle East* (University of California Press, 1988); and "Peace and Palestine: The Road That Is Not Straight," *The Economist*, vol. 322 (January 25, 1992), pp. 40–42.

56. The central objective of "strategic parity" was to expand the Syrian military to the point where it could effectively deter Israeli attack. But it is worth noting that the doctrine also had an explicit economic dimension, aimed at beefing up Syria's industrial capacity and technological skills to match Israel's. See Ahmed S. Khalidi and Hussein Agha, "The Syrian Doctrine of Strategic Parity," in Judith Kipper and Harold H. Saunders, eds., *The Middle East in Global Perspective* (Boulder, Colo.: Westview Press, 1991), pp. 186–218; and Kassem M. Ja'far, "Syria's Military Build-up after June 1982: Implications for the Future of the Arab-Israeli Balance," *RUSI & Brassey's Defence Yearbook, 1988* (London: Brassey's, 1988), pp. 171–96.

57. American Embassy, Commercial Section, *Syria's Commercial Setting and Trends* (September 13, 1991); and Robert Fisk, "Exasperated Moscow Wants Its Ties with Syria on a New Footing," *The Independent*, July 6, 1989, p. 11.

58. "Syria: Soviet Factor behind 1989 Trade Miracle," *MEED*, October 12, 1990, p. 23.

59. "For Syrians, Box of Salt is No Longer Big Luxury," *Jerusalem Post*, March 26, 1991, p. 6; and "Syria: The Price of Liberalizing," *The Middle East*, no. 203 (September 1991), pp. 20–21.

CHAPTER 4

1. Janne E. Nolan, "The Conventional Arms Market after Iraq: Prospects for Control," *Disarmament*, vol. 14 (1991), p. 19.

2. "It would take 10 Iraqi al-Husayn missiles, which have warheads of only 180–190 kg of explosives, to equal the payload carried by a single F-16"; W. Seth Carus, "Missiles in the Middle East: A New Threat to Stability," *Policy Focus* (Washington Institute for Near East Policy), no. 6 (June 1988), p. 7. See also Andrew Hull, "The Role of Ballistic Missiles in Third World Defence Strategies," *Jane's Intelligence Review*, vol. 3 (October 1991), pp. 464–70. For an Arab perspective, see "Alaf Al-Sawarikh fil-Sharq al-Awsat Tuthir Qalaq al-Duwal al-Kubra" (Thousands of missiles in the Middle East stir the anxiety of the big powers), *al-Wasat*, March 23, 1922, pp. 24–26. For an authoritative treatment of this subject, see Janne E. Nolan, *Trappings of Power: Ballistic Missiles in the Third World* (Brookings, 1991).

3. The entry costs of a missile program seem to be much lower than those of acquiring advanced fighter bombers. Reports suggest that Syria may be paying North Korea $500 million for 150 Scud-C missiles. Compare this to the $9 billion that Saudi Arabia is paying the United States for 72 F-15s. Of course, even $500 million stretches the budgets of the poorer Arab states. The Iraqis, too, tried to augment their arsenal by purchasing Scud-Cs from North Korea during the Gulf War, but Pyongyang denied the request because Baghdad lacked the cash to make immediate payment on the sale. See Steven Emerson, "The Postwar Scud Boom," *Wall Street Journal*, July 10, 1991, p. A12.

4. This approach has been adopted in Israel (see chapter 5) and perhaps in Iraq; see Ehud Ya'ari, "Iraq's New Order of Battle," *Jerusalem Report*, July 4, 1991, p. 36.

5. For a discussion of the effect of downsizing the armed forces, see S. B. L. Kapoor, "Cutting the Army Down to Size—A Large Standing Army vs a Small, Mobile, Hard-hitting Force," *Indian Defense Review*, July 1988, pp. 76–84.

6. On the Mubarak plan and its antecedents, see Mahmoud Karem, *A Nuclear-Weapons-Free Zone in the Middle East: Problems and Prospects* (Westport, Conn.: Greenwood Press, 1988); Mohamed Nabil Fahmy, "Egypt's Disarmament Initiative," *Bulletin of the Atomic Scientists*, vol. 46 (November 1990), pp. 9–10; and UN General Assembly, *Establishment of a Nuclear-Weapon-Free Zone in the Region of the Middle East*, A/45/435, October 10, 1990.

7. Yoram Nimrod, "Arms Control or Arms Race?" *New Outlook*, September–October 1991, p. 17.

8. Kenneth R. Timmerman, *The Death Lobby: How the West Armed Iraq* (Houghton Mifflin, 1991), p. 33.

9. R. Jeffrey Smith and Glenn Frankel, "Saddam's Nuclear-Weapons Dream: A Lingering Nightmare," *Washington Post*, October 13, 1991, p. A44.

10. "By-ways That Lead to the Bomb," *The Economist*, July 20, 1991, pp. 101–02. For the Israeli campaign against Iraq's nuclear weapons program, see Steve Weissman and Herbert Krosney, *The Islamic Bomb: The Nuclear Threat to Israel and the Middle East* (Times Books, 1981), chapters 4 and 5.

11. Baghdad had a third nuclear program based on chemical enrichment of uranium as well, but that program was not nearly as well funded as the other two.

12. Thomas Land, "Saddam's Hidden Nuclear Bid," *South*, September–October 1991, pp. 15–17; and UN Security Council, *Consolidated Report on the First Two IAEA Inspections under Security Council Resolution 687 (1991) of Iraqi Nuclear Capabilities* (International Atomic Energy Agency, July 11, 1991), p. 11.

13. David Albright and Mark Hibbs, "Iraq's Nuclear Hide-and-Seek," *Bulletin of the Atomic Scientists*, vol. 47 (September 1991), pp. 14–23; and David Albright and Mark Hibbs, "Iraq's Bomb: Blueprints and Artifacts," *Bulletin of the Atomic Scientists*, vol. 48 (January–February 1992), pp. 39–40.

14. Frederick Kempe, "Germans Had Big Role in Helping Iraq Arm, Internal Report Shows," *Wall Street Journal*, October 2, 1990, p. A1; and R. Jeffrey Smith, "Long-Term Crackdown on Iraq Faces Obstacles," *Washington Post*, September 20, 1990, p. A27.

15. Alan George, "Saddam's Supply Routes," *The Middle East*, no. 198 (April 1991), pp. 20–22; Richard Donkin, "Network of Companies with Baghdad Ties," *Financial Times*, September 21, 1989, p. 6; and Victor Mallet and others, "West Supplied Iraqi Bomb-Makers," *Financial Times*, October 4, 1991, p. 4.

16. UN Security Council, *Report on the Fourth IAEA On-Site Inspection in Iraq under Security Council Resolution 687 (1991)*, S/22986 (United Nations, August 28, 1991).

17. Mark Hibbs of *Nucleonics Week* and Betsy Perabo of the Monterey Institute of International Studies supplied invaluable information for these estimates. See also Jonathan Broder, "Saddam Hussein's Bomb Is Still Ticking," *Jerusalem Report*, February 6, 1992, p. 13.

18. The most reliable assessments of the Iraqi nuclear program can be found in a series of articles by David Albright and Mark Hibbs, including "Iraq and the Bomb: Were They Even Close?" *Bulletin of the Atomic Scientists*, vol. 47 (March 1991), pp. 16–25; "Hyping the Iraqi Bomb," *Bulletin of the Atomic Scientists*, vol. 47 (March 1991), pp. 26–28; and "Iraq's Bomb: Blueprints and Artifacts," cited in n. 13. See also Albright and Hibbs, "Iraq's Quest for the Nuclear Grail: What Can We Learn?" *Arms Control Today* (July–August 1992), pp. 3–11.

19. See Anthony H. Cordesman, *Weapons of Mass Destruction in the Middle East* (London: Brassey's, 1991); and Leonard S. Spector, "Nuclear Proliferation in the Middle East," *Orbis*, vol. 36 (Spring 1992), pp. 181–98. It is not inconceivable that an Arab state might buy a bomb "off the shelf" from an existing nuclear power. This would certainly be the most economical approach. However, none of the existing nuclear powers—even those such as North Korea, Kazakhstan, or Pakistan, which have close ties to Arab states—seems ready to risk the international opprobrium and strategic complications that might accompany such a sale.

20. Middle-income Arab states such as Syria, Algeria, or Libya would be hard pressed today to finance a nuclear weapons program even if they could overcome the inefficiencies of the Iraqi nuclear program. Iraqi scientists had never produced a bomb before; they were not so much trying to build a bomb

as to invent one. If they had known what they were doing and exactly which techniques worked, they could have saved much costly experimentation. The prospect of nuclear scientists from the former Soviet Union seeking more lucrative employment in the third world has thus raised fears that future bomb-building efforts may be much more efficient; see "Libyans Said to Woo Russian Atom Scientists," *Washington Post*, January 9, 1992, p. A37; and "Ba'd 'Asifat al-Sahra': Hal Ma Zala Saddam Yamluk al-Qunbula al-Dhariyya?" (After Desert Storm: Does Saddam still have the nuclear bomb?), *al-Majalla*, February 26–March 3, 1992, pp. 46–48.

However, even with the advantage of technical expertise, nuclear weapons are not cheap. Using a breeder reactor to generate weapons-grade plutonium, a nuclear device can be built for under a billion dollars, but, as the Iraqis discovered, this approach is hard to conceal and likely to provoke an international reaction. The most secure and effective way to build a bomb may be to employ centrifuges to enrich uranium, but a ten-year program to do this would cost around $5 billion. Even though this amount is far less than the Iraqis spent, it would represent a massive investment for a middle-income Arab state.

The author wishes to thank Gary Milhollin of the Wisconsin Project on Nuclear Disarmament for sharing his expertise on the technical costs of weapons development.

21. Seymour M. Hersh, *The Samson Option: Israel's Nuclear Arsenal and American Foreign Policy* (Random House, 1991), pp. 198–200.

22. R. Jeffrey Smith, "Gates Warns of Iranian Arms Drive," *Washington Post*, March 29, 1992, p. A1.

23. Yezid Sayigh, "Reversing the Middle East Nuclear Race," *Middle East Report*, vol. 22 (July–August 1992), pp. 14–19.

24. Even ostensibly "radical" states such as Syria support the proposal; see Yoram Nimrod, "Arms Control or Arms Race?" *New Outlook*, vol. 34 (September–October 1991), pp. 15–18.

25. James M. Markham, "Arabs Link Curbs on Gas and A-Arms," *New York Times*, January 8, 1989, p. A8; and "Chemical Arms Ban Still Uncertain," *Science*, vol. 243 (January 20, 1989), pp. 301–02.

26. See W. Seth Carus, "Chemical Weapons in the Middle East," *Policy Focus*, no. 9 (December 1988); Elisa D. Harris, "Stemming the Spread of Chemical Weapons," *Brookings Review*, vol. 8 (Winter 1989–90), pp. 39–45; and "Li-Madha Lam Yustakhdam al-'Iraq al-Asliha al-Kimawiyya?" (Why didn't Iraq use chemical weapons?), *al-Majalla*, February 26–March 3, 1992, pp. 32–34.

27. The May 1992 Bush proposal called for all states in the region to prohibit the production of nuclear weapons, which would have capped Israel's arsenal but left it intact. This feature led to Syrian and Iranian criticism of the proposal. See Syrian Arab Television, June 2, 1991, in Foreign Broadcast Information Service, *Daily Report: Near East and South Asia*, June 3, 1991, p. 42 (hereafter FBIS, *Near East*); and Voice of the Islamic Republic of Iran First Program, in FBIS, *Near East*, June 4, 1991, p. 26. Although Iran and Syria objected in principle to legitimation of Israel's regional nuclear monopoly, neither country

was likely to directly challenge that monopoly in the near future. Despite rumors that both countries were interested in acquiring nuclear weapons, Syria had only a tiny nuclear program, and Iran, although it had more advanced technical capabilities, had not yet taken definitive steps toward nuclear weapons research. Both countries cooperated fully with International Atomic Energy Agency inspections in 1992 that determined that neither country was engaged in weapons research. See R. Jeffrey Smith, "Officials Say Iran Is Seeking Nuclear Weapons Capability," *Washington Post*, October 30, 1991, p. A1; "Iran: Iran 'Has No Need' for Nuclear Weapons," *Middle East Economic Digest*, December 6, 1991, p. 16 (hereafter *MEED*); Michael Z. Weiss, "Atomic Team Reports on Iran Probe," *Washington Post*, February 25, 1992, p. A29; and Jon Wolfsthal, "Iran Hosts IAEA Mission; Syria Signs Safeguard Pact," *Arms Control Today*, vol. 22 (March 1992), p. 28.

28. See Shai Feldman, *Israeli Nuclear Deterrence* (Columbia University Press, 1982); Yohanan Ramati, "Israel and Nuclear Deterrence," *Global Affairs*, vol. 3 (Spring 1988), pp. 175–85; and Avner Cohen and Marvin Miller, "Nuclear Shadows in the Middle East: Prospects for Arms Control in the Wake of the Gulf Crisis," Defense and Arms Control Studies Working Paper (Massachusetts Institute of Technology, December 1990).

29. For a survey of this debate, by a Palestinian intellectual who is critical of the idea of accepting an Israeli nuclear monopoly, see Yazid Sayigh, "al-Jidal al-Nawawi fi Isra'il" (The nuclear debate in Israel), *Shu'un Filastiniyya*, no. 189 (December 1988), pp. 51–61.

30. For a survey of these measures, see Ahmad Khalidi, "Middle East Security: Arab Threat Perceptions, Peace, and Stability," in *Middle East Security: Two Views*, Occasional Paper no. 3 (International Security Studies Program, American Academy of Arts and Sciences, May 1990), pp. 1–21.

31. The 1992 budget is outlined in *al-Ra'y*, December 12, 1991, in FBIS, *Near East*, December 24, 1991, pp. 37–44.

32. "Jordan: Mirage Cancellation Talks Continue," *MEED*, September 6, 1991, p. 22.

33. Philip Finnegan, "Jordan Cuts Armed Forces; Plans to Sell Off Aircraft," *Defense News*, vol. 6 (November 25, 1991), pp. 1, 22; and E. Y. [Ehud Ya'ari], "Less Guns and Butter," *Jerusalem Report*, March 12, 1992, p. 26.

34. "'Amman: Khatwa Jadida li-Khafd al-Anfaq al-'Askari" (Amman: A new step to reduce military expenditure), *al-Wasat*, March 16, 1992, p. 4.

35. E. Y., "Less Guns and Butter."

36. "Jordan's Military Chief Eager to Resume Ties with U.S., Defense Role during War," *Inside the Army*, February 17, 1992, pp. 3, 10.

37. For a useful introduction to the CSCE process, see Jonathan Dean, *Meeting Gorbachev's Challenge* (St. Martin's Press, 1989).

38. Hermann Scheer, *Disarmament in the Mediterranean instead of Rapid Reaction Forces: A Concept for a New All-European Security* (Bonn: Bundeshaus, April 1992), p. 6.

39. *The Gulf Crisis: Incremental Financial Impact on Jordan and Regional Security* (Amman, November 1990).

40. *Looking Beyond the Gulf War: A Conference on Security and Cooperation in the Middle East* (Amman, March 1991), pp. 14–15.

41. Hugh Carnegy and Lamis Andoni, "Jordan Sees Economic Disaster," *Financial Times*, September 3, 1990, p. 2; and Pamela Dougherty and Simon Edge, "Jordan Heads for the Rocks," *MEED*, September 14, 1990, pp. 4–5.

42. Alan Cowell, "5 Are Killed in South Jordan as Rioting over Food Prices Spreads," *New York Times*, April 20, 1989, p. A3; and Pamela Dougherty and Simon Edge, "Amman Attempts to Strike a Balance," *MEED*, December 15, 1989, pp. 4–5.

43. For a study of several such "IMF riots" in the Arab world, see David Seddon, "Riot and Rebellion in North Africa: Political Responses to Economic Crisis in Tunisia, Morocco, and Sudan," in Berch Berberoglu, ed., *Power and Stability in the Middle East* (London: Zed Books, 1989), pp. 114–35.

44. J. Eugene Gibson and William J. Schrenk, "The Enterprise for the Americas Initiative: A Second Generation of Debt-for-Nature Exchanges—with an Overview of Other Recent Exchange Initiatives," *George Washington Journal of International Law and Economics*, vol. 25, no. 1 (1991), pp. 1–70.

45. This was the idea underlying the so-called Baker Plan, which had used it to justify offering indebted countries only debt rescheduling rather than debt relief. See Robin Broad, "How About a Real Solution to Third World Debt?" *New York Times*, September 28, 1987, p. A25.

46. For a discussion of this issue, focused on how the threat of default on American military debts strained relations between Cairo and Washington, see William B. Quandt, *The United States and Egypt* (Brookings, 1990).

47. Steven Greenhouse, "Half of Egypt's $20.2 Billion Debt Being Forgiven by U.S. and Allies," *New York Times*, May 27, 1991, p. 1; and "Yemen: Paris Strikes Off Debt," *MEED*, September 28, 1990, p. 32.

48. In fact, the text of the actual Jordanian proposal does not call for industrialized creditor states to shoulder the burden of debt forgiveness alone. It urges the wealthier, relatively debt-free Arab states to contribute too by buying part of the debts of their poorer neighbors.

49. Daniel P. Hewitt, "Military Expenditure: International Comparison of Trends," IMF Working Paper, WP/91/54 (Washington: Fiscal Affairs Department, International Monetary Fund, 1991). See also Daniel P. Hewitt, "Military Expenditures in the Developing World," *Finance and Development*, vol. 28 (September 1991), pp. 22–25.

50. Paula De Masi and Henri Lorie, "How Resilient Are Military Expenditures?" *International Monetary Fund Staff Papers*, vol. 36 (March 1989), pp. 130–65.

51. Lionel Barber and Michael Prowse, "IMF Chief Backs Call to Limit Arms Sales," *Financial Times*, March 20, 1991, p. 16.

52. Paul Blustein, "World Bank, IMF to Press Defense Cuts," *Washington Post*, October 18, 1991, pp. B1, B4.

53. "Asbab Takhfid al-Jaysh al-Yamani" (Reasons for the reduction of the Yemeni army), *al-Majalla*, August 5–11, 1992, p. 23; and "Bud' Khafd 'Addad

Afrad al-Jaysh al-Yamani" (The start of reductions of troop numbers of the Yemeni army), *al-Wasat*, August 10, 1992, p. 5.

54. The *locus classicus* for collective security is Independent Commission on Disarmament and Security Issues, *Common Security: A Blueprint for Survival* (Simon and Schuster, 1982).

55. "GCC Plans Defence Force," *MEED*, September 6, 1991, p. 10; and "Who Guards the Gulf," *The Economist*, September 7, 1991, p. 41.

56. Gerald Butt, "The Damascus Declaration: Eight Pairs of Eyes on Iraq," *Middle East International*, March 22, 1991, pp. 9–10; and Rida al-Laythi, "Qira'a fi I'lan Dimashq" (A reading of the Damascus Declaration), *al-Ahram al-Iqtisadi*, March 18, 1991, p. 62.

57. David B. Ottaway, "Aid to Egypt, Syria Tied to Free Markets," *Washington Post*, April 6, 1991, pp. A15, A16; "GCC Fund Approved," *MEED*, May 3, 1991, p. 6; and Abdel-Ati Mohamed, "$10 Billion Arab Aid Fund," *al-Ahram Weekly*, December 26, 1991, p. 1.

58. Michael R. Gordon, "Network of Bases," *New York Times*, September 4, 1990, pp. A1, A9.

59. Patrick E. Tyler, "U.S. and Bahrain Near Pact on Permanent Military Base," *New York Times*, March 25, 1991, p. A9; Michael R. Gordon, "Cheney Reports Gulf Accepting a U.S. Presence," *New York Times*, May 10, 1991, pp. A1, A10; Nadim Jaber, "Conflicting Visions," *Middle East International*, November 22, 1991, pp. 12–13; and Eric Schmitt, "U.S. Negotiating New Security Pacts in Gulf," *New York Times*, August 1, 1991, p. A6.

60. David B. Ottaway, "Kuwaitis Hint at Long U.S. Presence," *Washington Post*, September 8, 1990, p. A18; Don Oberdorfer, "Cheney Says Security Should Rest with Arabs," *Washington Post*, February 25, 1991, p. A11; and Barton Gellman, "U.S., Kuwait Initial Security Accord," *Washington Post*, September 6, 1991, p. A24.

61. *KUNA*, October 2, 1991, in FBIS, *Near East*, October 4, 1991, p. 9; and *KUNA*, October 12, 1991, in FBIS, *Near East*, October 15, 1991, p. 13.

62. David Hoffman, "Baker Proposes New Alliance to Contain Iraqi Aggression," *Washington Post*, September 5, 1990, p. 1. Although criticism forced Baker to downplay this plan during the following weeks, it emerged once again in the "regional security" recommendations of the Gates working group; see "Waging the Peace," *Middle East Policy Survey*, no. 264 (February 1, 1991); and Theresa Hitchens and George Leopold, "Allies Ponder Gulf Security," *Defense News*, March 4, 1991, pp. 1, 28.

63. The rationale for Saudi opposition to collective security arrangements is discussed in detail in chapter 5.

64. For a survey of possible approaches, see Shelly A. Stahl and Geoffrey Kemp, eds., *Arms Control and Weapons Proliferation in the Middle East and South Asia* (St. Martin's Press, 1992); and Dore Gold, ed., *Arms Control in the Middle East* (Boulder, Colo.: Westview Press, 1991).

CHAPTER 5

1. For a mathematical analysis which suggests that these three states have played the leading role in promoting the regional arms race, see Robert E. Looney, "Arms Races in the Middle East: A Test of Causality," *Arms Control*, vol. 11 (September 1990), pp. 178–90.

2. Israel's partisans have worked hard to present the country as a tiny David facing a Goliath Arab military machine. In fact, however, virtually all experts—including the U.S. Department of Defense—believe the Israel Defense Forces have always been more than a match for their Arab neighbors. See Alon Pinkas, "American Rejection of More Military Aid No Surprise," *Jerusalem Post*, October 9, 1991, p. 1.

3. Yoram Peri, "Coexistence or Hegemony? Shifts in the Israeli Security Concept," in Dan Caspi and Emanuel Gutmann, eds., *The Roots of Begin's Success: The 1981 Israeli Elections* (St. Martin's Press, 1983), pp. 191–216.

4. Ironically, American foreign aid has fostered the same trends in Israel that oil has encouraged in Arab states: private-sector dependence on public subsidies, government reliance on patronage, and a general mismatch between consumption patterns and the productivity of the local economy.

5. Joel Bainerman, "Cut Off Aid to Israel and Watch It Thrive," *Wall Street Journal*, July 23, 1991, p. A22.

6. Hugh Carnegy, "The Chinks in Shamir's Armor," *Financial Times*, June 20, 1991, p. 16; and Amy Dockser Marcus, "Israel Declares It Can Still Raise Capital despite U.S. Refusal of Loan Guarantees," *Wall Street Journal*, March 23, 1992, p. A7.

7. Amy Dockser Marcus, "Rabin Readies Plans for the Reform of Israel's Sick Economy, amid Doubts," *Wall Street Journal*, July 7, 1992, p. A10.

8. Emma Murphy, "Can Rabin Reform Israel's Economy?" *Middle East International*, July 10, 1992, p. 18; and Amy Dockser Marcus, "Israel Government May End Up Owning Nation's Biggest Banks," *Wall Street Journal*, September 29, 1992, p. A12.

9. Hugh Carnegy, "Israel Conscious of Weak Card among Its Aces," *Financial Times*, October 31, 1991, p. 4.

10. Marcus, "Israel Declares It Can Still Raise Capital," p. A7; and Jackson Diehl, "Israeli Proposes 8-Year Plan for U.S. Economic Aid Cutoff," *Washington Post*, November 26, 1991, p. A14.

11. Diehl, "Israeli Proposes 8-Year Plan," p. A14; and Marit Gilat, "A Cure for Aid?" *Jerusalem Report*, December 12, 1991, p. 23.

12. Neal Sandler, "The Big Sell," *Jerusalem Report*, March 26, 1992, pp. 18–21; and Hugh Carnegy, "Israeli Chorus for Privatisation Sets Labour's Agenda," *Financial Times*, July 8, 1992, p. 6.

13. Amy Dockser Marcus, "Public Debate Emerges as Israel Seeks to Reduce Its Dependence on U.S. Aid," *Wall Street Journal*, December 12, 1991, p. A11.

14. Shimon Peres, "Israeli Security in a New Age," *Jerusalem Post*, September 6, 1991, p. 9.

15. Neal Sandler, "A Pared-down IDF," *Jerusalem Report*, June 20, 1991, p. 16.

16. Barbara Opall, "Israel Eyes 40 Percent Aid Hike," *Defense News*, September 9, 1991, pp. 4, 44. While the dollar value of U.S. military assistance had remained constant, Congress had arranged to increase its utility through a variety of subterfuges. The aid was paid out to Israel in a single tranche at the beginning of the year, allowing Jerusalem to earn interest on it. American military equipment sold to Israel was assigned a lower price than equipment sold to other countries. Some American military assistance, such as funding for Israel's Arrow antiballistic missile and for pre-positioning American equipment in Israel, was not counted against the $3 billion total but was drawn from other elements of the U.S. budget. See Edward T. Pound, "A Close Look at U.S. Aid to Israel Reveals Deals That Push Cost above Publicly Quoted Figures," *Wall Street Journal*, September 19, 1991, p. A16.

17. Y. K. H. [Yossi Klein Halevi], "Keeping Track of Mother's Money," *Jerusalem Report*, July 11, 1991, p. 14.

18. ."Burnishing Israel's Arrow," *The Economist*, July 28, 1990, p. 34.

18. "Israeli CoS in Funding Dispute," *Jane's Defence Weekly*, September 7, 1991, p. 385; and "Tel Aviv University press release," Government Press Office (Jerusalem), September 4, 1991, in Foreign Broadcast Information Service, *Daily Report: Near East and South Asia*, September 9, 1991, p. 27 (hereafter FBIS, *Near East*).

20. *Ha'aertz*, December 11, 1991, in FBIS, *Near East*, December 11, 1991, p. 46.

21. Ron Ben-Yishay, "Generals versus the Political Echelon," *Yedi'ot Aharonot*, December 27, 1991, in FBIS, *Near East*, December 24, 1991, p. 17.

22. Barbara Opall, "Israeli Ministries Part Paths on Military Budget Plans," *Defense News*, August 19, 1991, pp. 1, 20.

23. Sandler, "A Pared-down IDF," p. 16; and Opall, "Israeli Ministries Part Paths," pp. 1, 20. For an overview of recent attempts by the Israeli military to cope with restraints on its budget, see "Israel Bites the Bullet on Defence Spending," *RUSI Journal*, vol. 12 (August 1992), pp. 61–63.

24. Eric Silver, "A Warrior for the Nineties," *Jerusalem Report*, June 20, 1991, pp. 12–16.

25. Bank of Israel, *Annual Report, 1990* (Jerusalem, May 1991), p. 149.

26. Some Israelis have worried that the loan guarantees proffered by Washington would actually damage the Israeli economy by encouraging fiscal irresponsibility. See Peretz Kidron, "The Loan Guarantees: A Boost or a Burden?" *Middle East International*, August 21, 1992, p. 5; and Amy Dockser Marcus, "Some Israelis Say Loan Guarantees May Be Harmful to the Economy," *Wall Street Journal*, August 13, 1992, p. A11.

27. Kamran Mofid, *The Economic Consequences of the Gulf War* (London: Routledge, 1990), p. 127.

28. International Monetary Fund (IMF), *International Financial Statistics Yearbook* (Washington, 1989), p. 421; and IMF, *International Financial Statistics* (Washington, April 1992), p. 292.

29. For example, see Patrick E. Tyler, "Hostages Go Free at Last, but Iran Bears Watching," *New York Times*, December 8, 1991, p. 1; and Ilyas Harfush, "Iran: Ta'ayyush al-Tayyarat al-Mutasari'a Rahna bi-Istimrar al-Khumayni" (Iran: The coexistence of the contradictory trends is dependent upon the continuation of Khomeini), *al-Majalla*, February 8–14, 1989, p. 21.

30. Don Oberdorfer, "Iran Paid for Release of Hostages," *Washington Post*, January 19, 1992, pp. A1, A21; and Ehud Ya'ari, "Where Have All the Iranians Gone?" *Jerusalem Report*, March 5, 1992, p. 30.

31. International Institute for Strategic Studies, *The Military Balance, 1990–1991* (London: Brassey's, 1990), pp. 103–06.

32. Geraldine Brooks, "The New Revolution in Iran Is Taking Place on an Economic Front," *Wall Street Journal*, September 16, 1991, p. A15.

33. *Middle East Economic Digest*, February 7, 1992, p. 13. (Hereafter *MEED.*)

34. Vahe Petrossian, "Iran: Rafsanjani Plan Cleared by Majlis," *MEED*, January 19, 1990, p. 14; and "Iran: Five-Year Plan under Urgent Review," *MEED*, September 29, 1990, p. 23.

35. "Rafsanjani Defends Price Rises amid Protests," *MEED*, July 26, 1991, pp. 2–13; and Caryle Murphy, "Vote in Iran Focuses on Economy," *Washington Post*, April 10, 1992, p. A46.

36. Fahmi Huwaydi, " 'Umm al-Ma'arik' al-Intikhabiyya fi Iran" (The 'Mother of all election battles' in Iran), *al-Majalla*, March 18–24, 1992, pp. 23–31; Caryle Murphy, "Hard-Liners Fall behind in Iran Vote," *Washington Post*, April 13, 1992, p. A1; and "Iran's Leader Gets Support in a Runoff," *New York Times*, May 10, 1992, p. 15.

37. Caryle Murphy, "Iran Pushes Postwar Reconstruction While Seeking Stable Ties with Iraq," *Washington Post*, April 16, 1992, p. 40; Tony Walker, "Gulf Leaders Edge towards Iran," *Financial Times*, December 24, 1990, p. 3; "Qatar, Saudi Arabia, and Iran: Balancing Act," *Issues: Perspectives on Middle East and World Affairs*, vol. 1 (December 1991), p. 1; and Fahmi Huwaydi, "al-'Alaqat al-Khalijiyya al-Iraniyya: Ila Ayn?" (Whither Gulf-Iranian relations?) *al-Shira'*, December 23, 1991, pp. 38–39.

38. "Air Force Commander Makes Moscow Mission," *MEED*, July 19, 1991, p. 18; and "Arms Deals with Russia Worth $5 Billion," *Sawt al-Kuwayt al-Duwali*, January 12, 1992, in FBIS, *Near East*, January 16, 1992, p. 40.

39. "Iran: Ukraine Receives Oil and Gas in $7,000 Million Barter," *MEED*, February 14, 1992, p. 21; and Mohammed Ziarati, "Iranian National Security Policy," *Middle East International*, April 3, 1992, pp. 18–19.

40. Gerald F. Seib, "Iran Is Re-Emerging as a Mideast Power as Iraqi Threat Fades," *Wall Street Journal*, March 18, 1992, p. A1.

41. "Proliferation Testimony for Sen. Glenn's Government Affairs Committee on 15 January," p. 6.

42. Lally Weymouth, "Iran Resurgent," *Washington Post*, April 10, 1992, p. A27.

43. Scheherazade Daneshkhu, "Iran Presses on with Campaign to Rebuild Its Military Might," *Financial Times*, February 6, 1992, p. 4.

44. International Institute for Strategic Studies, *The Military Balance, 1991– 1992* (London: Brassey's, 1991), p. 105.

45. Elaine Sciolino, "Counting Iran's New Arms Is the Easy Part," *New York Times*, April 26, 1992, p. 2.

46. David Hoffman, "Iran's Rebuilding Seen as Challenge to West," *Washington Post*, February 2, 1992, p. A25.

47. Robert Pear, "Arms Sales to Third World Said to Decline Sharply," *New York Times*, June 21, 1990, p. A10.

48. For an analysis of the forces that have historically frustrated collective security in the Gulf, see Thomas L. McNaugher, *Arms and Oil* (Brookings, 1985), pp. 127–59; and J. E. Peterson, "Security Concerns in the Arabian Peninsula," in M. E. Ahrari, ed., *The Gulf and International Security* (St. Martin's, 1989), pp. 101–26.

49. For Saudi domestic politics, see Ghassane Salameh, "Political Power and the Saudi State," MERIP Reports, no. 91 (October 1980), pp. 5–23; Ayman al-Yassini, *Religion and State in the Kingdom of Saudi Arabia* (Boulder, Colo.: Westview Press, 1985); and Peter Theroux, "King Fahd's Big Gamble," *Vanity Fair*, vol. 54 (April 1991), pp. 126–34.

50. David B. Ottaway, "Combating a Cultural Clash," *Washington Post*, September 13, 1990, p. A33. See also the wonderful article, "Touchy Topics in the Gulf," *Harper's*, vol. 281 (November 1990), pp. 18–19.

51. Victor Mallet, "Saudi Arabian Media Seize an Opportunity to Tell It Like It Is," *Financial Times*, August 20, 1990, p. 3.

52. Lara Marlowe, "Saudi Arabia's Shias Now Face Test of Loyalty," *Financial Times*, September 13, 1990, p. 2; and Geraldine Brooks, "Shiites in Gulf States See Opportunity in Crisis," *Wall Street Journal*, November 16, 1990, p. A12.

53. Faysal Jalul, "Tuzahirat al-Riyadh al-Nisa'iyya Tarahat al-Qadiya: Hal Yajuz lil-Mar'a Qiyadat al-Sayyara?" (Demonstration by women in Riyadh poses the question: Is it permissible for women to drive cars?), *al-Yawm al-Sabi'*, December 2, 1990, pp. 14–16; and Youssef M. Ibrahim, "Saudi Women Take Driver's Seat in Protest," *New York Times*, November 7, 1990, p. A18.

54. "The Saudis' World Asunder," *The Economist*, January 26, 1991, pp. 20–21; see also David B. Ottaway, "Saudi Liberals See Reforms Unlikely," *Washington Post*, April 16, 1991, pp. A1, A14. The *Mutawwa'in* function as the religious police in the kingdom, enforcing attendance at prayers, Islamic dress, and the ban on alcohol and smoking; see Michael Field, "Stirring Religious Pride and Prejudice in Saudi Arabia," *Financial Times*, January 29, 1991, p. 2.

55. Many, in fact, had been critical of the dynasty's decision to summon American troops to confront Iraq, contending that this decision was both politically unwise and brought "infidel" troops into the environs of Islam's most

holy cities. See Judith Caesar, "Liberals and Conservatives Press Riyadh," *New York Times*, July 5, 1991, p. 21.

56. *al-Sha'b*, May 21, 1991, in FBIS, *Near East*, May 23, 1991, pp. 21–22.

57. Safa Haeri, "Saudi Arabia: A Warning to the King," *Middle East International*, June 24, 1991, p. 11.

58. A second petition, circulated in August, contained even more scathing criticisms of the dynasty's policies; see "Explanatory Memorandum to King," *al-Quds al-'Arabi*, August 1, 1991, in FBIS, *Near East*, August 22, 1991, pp. 22–26. See also Andrew Apostolou, "Stirrings of Political Debate," *The Middle East*, no. 205 (November 1991), pp. 17–18; *al-Jumhuriyya*, November 23, 1991, in FBIS, *Near East*, November 26, 1991, pp. 17–18; Neil MacFarquhar, "Secret Tapes of Saudi Arabia," *Jerusalem Post*, January 3, 1992, p. 12; Youssef M. Ibrahim, "Saudi Rulers Are Confronting Challenge by Islamic Radicals," *New York Times*, March 9, 1992, pp. A1, A7; and Caryle Murphy, "Conservative Clergy Attack Saudi Government," *Washington Post*, September 28, 1992, p. A12.

59. Youssef M. Ibrahim, "Saudis Widen Military Recruiting and Encourage Women to Work," *New York Times*, September 5, 1990, p. A1.

60. Lara Marlowe, "A Shortage of Men," *Financial Times*, December 12, 1990, p. II.

61. David B. Ottaway, "U.S., Saudis to Study Long-Term Defense Needs of Gulf Region," *Washington Post*, April 21, 1991, p. A26.

62. Ian Kemp, "War for Kuwait: The Way They Won the War of Liberation," *MEED*, April 26,1991, pp. 11–12. For a detailed survey of Saudi arms purchases, see Muhammad Ziarati, "The Defence of Arabia after the Gulf War," *Middle East International*, February 7, 1992, pp. 19–20.

63. David Silverberg, "Official Says U.S. Likely to Sell Arms to Saudis Piecemeal," *Defense News*, July 22, 1991, p. 60. Later estimates were that the Saudis would spend $14 billion on upgrading their ground forces; see "Saudi Arms Gets Review," *Defense News*, August 26, 1991, p. 2.

64. John M. Goshko, "U.S. Near Sale of F-15 Jets to Saudis," *Washington Post*, January 24, 1992, p. A7.

65. William J. Perry, "Desert Storm and Deterrence," *Foreign Affairs*, vol. 70 (Fall 1990), p. 69. See also John Simpson, "Trends in the Proliferation of Sophisticated Weapons and Missile Technology and Their Implications for International and Regional Security," *Disarmament*, vol. 14 (1991), pp. 40–57.

66. For the concept of advanced conventional warfare, see Ashton B. Carter, William J. Perry, and John D. Steinbruner, *A New Concept of Cooperative Security* (Brookings, 1992), pp. 48–51.

67. R. Jeffrey Smith, "Administration Proposes Arms Package for Saudis," *Washington Post*, July 30, 1991, p. A12.

68. "USA, Saudi Agree on Joint Training," *Jane's Defence Weekly*, September 14, 1991, p. 452.

69. "al-Harb al-Jawiyya: Tafasil al-Darba al-Ula" (The air war: Details of the first strike), *al-Majalla*, February 26–March 3, 1992, pp. 35–37.

70. James E. Akins, "The New Arabia," *Foreign Affairs*, vol. 70 (Summer 1991), pp. 44–45; and M. B. [Marwan Bishara], "Saudi Arabia: The New Gulf Cop?" *Issues*, vol. 1 (January 1992), pp. 6–7.

71. "[Saudi] Staff Gen. Prince Khalid expressed his opinion that establishing a unified Gulf army at the present time might face a number of obstacles and that hastiness in this matter might 'lead to adverse results'"; see FBIS, *Near East*, February 27, 1992, pp. 27–28. See also Nadim Jaber, "Expectations Unmatched," *Middle East International*, January 10, 1992, pp. 10–11.

72. Hisham Milhim, Radio Monte Carlo, May 10, 1991, in FBIS, *Near East*, May 10, 1991, pp. 3–4; Caryle Murphy, "Egypt's Pullout Signals Discord with Gulf," *Washington Post*, May 11, 1991, p. 18; and Max Rodenbeck, "Why Mubarak Did a U-turn on the Gulf," *Middle East International*, May 17, 1991, p. 3. For the wider problems involved in coordinating security objectives between the Gulf states and their poorer neighbors, see Yezid Sayigh, "Regional Security in the Gulf: The Geopolitical Realities," *Middle East International*, May 31, 1991, pp.17–18.

73. David B. Ottaway, "U.S., Saudis to Study Long-Term Defense Needs of Gulf Region," *Washington Post*, April 21, 1991, p. A26; and Andy Pasztor, "Pentagon Plans on Permanent Presence in Gulf," *Wall Street Journal*, September 20, 1990, p. A4.

74. Patrick E. Tyler, "Gulf Security Talks Stall over Plan for Saudi Army," *New York Times*, October 13, 1991, pp. 1, 12; John Lancaster and David Hoffman, "U.S., Saudis at Odds over Arms Cache," *Washington Post*, October 20, 1991, pp. A1, A33; and "Security Arrangements—Over the Horizon II," *Middle East Policy Survey*, no. 267 (March 15, 1991).

75. Judith Miller, "Saudi General Sees No Need for Big American Presence," *New York Times*, April 29, 1991, p. 9; "Getting It Down on Paper," *Middle East Policy Survey*, no. 273 (July 1, 1991), pp. 2–3; and Richard H. P. Sia, "Arabs Spurn U.S. Umbrella," *Jerusalem Post*, July 31, 1991, p. 5. The Saudis refused to sign any new agreements with Washington and insisted that whatever arrangements were reached be portrayed as revisions to a 1977 military training mission treaty; see Don Oberdorfer, "U.S., Saudis Agree to Use Old Military Pact for Expanding Cooperation," *Washington Post*, May 31, 1992, p. A10.

76. Donald Neff, "The United States: An Empty Gesture," *Middle East International*, June 14, 1991, pp. 6–7; "UAE, Bahrain to Get Apache Gunships," *Jane's Defence Weekly*, June 15, 1991, p. 1001; and David Silverberg, "Bank Scandal Delays UAE Buy of M1A1," *Defense News*, July 29, 1991, pp. 1, 29.

77. William Hartung, "The Boom at the Arms Bazaar," *Bulletin of the Atomic Scientists*, vol. 47 (October 1991), pp. 14–20; and "Tuzahira Hashida min al-'Urud wal-Nadwat wal-Munawarat Hudur 400 Shirka min 42 Balad" (A crowded demonstration of displays, discussions, and maneuvers; 400 companies from 42 countries in attendance), *al-Majalla*, October 30–November 5, 1991, pp. 50–53.

78. Barbara Starr, "Middle Eastern Promise," *Jane's Defence Weekly*, October 26, 1991, pp. 767–68.

79. "Kuwait: Budget Set for Record Deficit," *MEED*, January 17, 1992, p. 15; and Mark Nicholson, "Kuwait's Defense Spending Expected to Increase Sharply," *Financial Times*, January 7, 1992, p. 4.

80. Amy Borrus, "Shut Down the Mideast Arms Bazaar? Forget It," *Business Week*, March 11, 1991, p. 28.

81. For the role of advanced conventional weapons in Israeli military doctrine, see Hirsh Goodman and W. Seth Carus, *The Future Battlefield and the Arab-Israeli Conflict* (New Brunswick, N.J.: Transaction Publishers, 1990).

82. See "Tel Aviv University press release."

83. Seib, "Iran is Re-Emerging as a Mideast Power," pp. A1, A10.

84. "No End to Arms Sales," *The Middle East*, no. 200 (June 1991), pp. 16–18.

85. Philip Finnegan, "Bahrain Upgrade Persists amid Cash Woes," *Defense News*, March 16, 1992, pp. 6–14.

86. Youssef M. Ibrahim, "Rulers of Kuwait on Spending Spree, Raising Debt Fears," *New York Times*, May 4, 1992, pp. A1, A6; and Craig Forman, "Kuwait Juggles Needs for Cash, Overseas Assets," *Wall Street Journal*, June 5, 1991, p. A9.

87. Philip Finnegan, "Kuwait Soon to Decide on New Tank, Fighter Planes," *Defense News*, March 16, 1992, p. 8.

88. Patrick Tyler, "Cheney Wants No Limit on Arms Sales for Gulf Allies," *New York Times*, March 20, 1991, p. 13.

89. "Saudis Shelve Plan to Seek Purchase of F-15 Fighters," *Wall Street Journal*, November 25, 1991, p. A14; and Leslie H. Gelb, "Trashing the Saudis," *New York Times*, April 24, 1992, p. A35.

90. David White and Victor Mallet, "UK Seeks £1bn from Saudis on Arms Deal," *Financial Times*, June 8–9, 1991, p. 22; "Saudi Black Hawk Buy Threatened," *Jane's Defence Weekly*, November 16, 1991, p. 927; and "Saudi Arabia: al-Yamamah Gets Cash Injection," *MEED*, April 17, 1992, p. 22.

91. Giovanni de Briganti, "Gulf Nations Stall Weapons Purchases," *Defense News*, March 16, 1992, p. 12.

92. "Saudi Banks Help Fund Defense Deal," *Financial Times*, April 13, 1992, p. 5; Daniel Green, "BAe Shrugs Off Saudi Move to Defer £8bn Air Base Project," *Financial Times*, August 24, 1992, p. 1; and David Pallister, "£40bn Saudi Defence Deal at Risk," *Guardian Weekly*, October 25, 1992, p. 9.

93. The relationship between dynast and subject in the *rentier* states of the Gulf is radically different from that which prevails in nation states. For a detailed description of this relationship, see Giacomo Luciani, *The Arab State* (University of California Press, 1990); and Khaldun Hasan al-Naqib, *al-Mujtama' wal-Dawla fil-Khalij wal-Jazira al-'Arabiyya* (Society and the state in the Gulf and the Arabian peninsula) (Beirut: Markaz Dirasat al-Wahda al-'Arabiyya, 1987).

94. The Bush initiative was originally conceived as an effort to stem the proliferation of weapons of mass destruction in the Middle East. In its original

draft, it made no reference to conventional weapons; its call for an arms suppliers' regime that might have controlled conventional weapons was added only at the last minute. See Ann Devroy, "President to Propose Mideast Arms Limits," *Washington Post*, April 27, 1991, p. 14. This narrow focus on WMDs helps to explain why the flood of sales to the Gulf triggered few alarms inside the administration.

95. Carroll J. Doherty, "The Dilemma of Mideast Arms Sales," *Congressional Quarterly*, vol. 49 (March 9, 1991), p. 614; and "U.S. Arms Transfers to Middle East Dampen Prospects for Paris Meeting," *Arms Control Today*, vol. 21 (July–August 1991), pp. 23, 31.

96. Don Oberdorfer and R. Jeffrey Smith, "U.S. Faces Contradiction on Mideast Arms Control," March 7, 1991, pp. A31, A33; and R. Jeffrey Smith, "U.S. Seen as Contributing to Arms Proliferation," *Washington Post*, June 21, 1991, p. A7. For an illuminating discussion of the forces that drive U.S. arms exports, see William D. Hartung, "Breaking the Arms-Sales Addiction: New Directions for U.S. Policy," *World Policy Journal*, vol. 8 (Winter 1990–91), pp. 1–26.

97. Robert Pear, "U.S. Sales of Arms to the Third World Declined by 22% Last Year," *New York Times*, July 21, 1992, p. A16.

98. Jackson Diehl and David von Drehle, "Bush Approves Sale of F-15s to Saudis," *Washington Post*, September 12, 1992, p. A1.

99. Eric Schmitt, "Kuwaitis Will Buy Tanks Made in U.S.," *New York Times*, October 13, 1992, p. A1.

100. Thomas L. Friedman, "U.S. and Israel Working Out Deal to Offset Warplane Sale to Saudis," *New York Times*, September 15, 1991, p. A1; Jackson Diehl, "Strategic Plans Giving Way to Mideast Arms Flow," *Washington Post*, October 4, 1992, p. A24; and Peretz Kidron, "Replenishing Israel's Arsenal," *Middle East International*, October 9, 1992, p. 3.

101. "U.S. Arms Transfers to Middle East Dampen Prospects for Paris Meeting," p. 23. See also Walter S. Mossberg and Rick Wartzman, "Mideast Arms Outlays Seem Unlikely to Face Any Tough New Curbs," *Wall Street Journal*, March 4, 1991, pp. A1, A6; and David Silverberg, "U.S. Arms Sales to Mideast Progress despite Bush Initiative," *Defense News*, June 3, 1991, p. 15.

102. "China has accused the West of having a double standard toward arms control, asserting that the United States and its allies do not want to limit their ability to sell aircraft, tanks and other conventional weapons to their friends in the area, and have drawn a distinction, in effect, between good arms sales and bad." In Elaine Sciolino, "Arms Vendors Fail to Impose Limits," *New York Times*, May 31, 1992, p. 12.

103. Patrick E. Tyler, "Gulf Security Talks Stall over Plan for Saudi Army," *New York Times*, October 13, 1991, p. 1; see also Ann Devroy, "President to Propose Mideast Arms Limits," *Washington Post*, April 27, 1991, p. 14.

104. "5 House Democrats Urge Mideast Arms Sale Curb," *Washington Post*, April 9, 1991, p. 17; Helen Dewar, "Congress Pressures Bush on Mideast Arms Curbs," *Washington Post*, May 15, 1991, p. 24; and Carroll J. Doherty, "Panel

Pushes to Cut Off Flow of Weapons to Middle East," *Congressional Quarterly*, vol. 49 (May 25, 1991), pp. 1390–91.

105. David Silverberg, "F-15, Tank Requests Stir U.S.-Saudi Relationship," *Defense News*, March 16, 1992, p. 14.

106. For a discussion of the political influence generated by a single sale, the 1981 Saudi acquisition of AWACs, see Steven Emerson, *The American House of Saud* (Franklin Watts, 1985), pp. 182–214. The success of this deal also greatly augmented the influence of the Saudi "point man" in Washington, Bandar bin Sultan, who was shortly afterward named ambassador to the United States; see Patrick E. Tyler, "Double Exposure: Saudi Arabia's Man in Washington," *New York Times Magazine*, June 7, 1992.

CHAPTER 6

1. The first effort in this direction was the Tripartite Declaration of 1950, in which the United States, Britain, and France agreed to halt arms sales to the Middle East; see Nadav Safran, *From War to War: The Arab-Israeli Confrontation, 1948–1967* (Pegasus, 1969), p. 48. The most recent effort is the Big Five talks.

2. Of course, supply-side controls may be useful in temporarily curbing the flow of arms or in restricting the proliferation of very high-technology weapons—such as nuclear devices—that only a handful of states can effectively produce.

3. For alternative proposals, see Alton Frye, "How We Can Contain the Mideast Arms Explosion," *Washington Post*, June 16, 1992, pp. B1, B5; David A. Koplow and Philip G. Schrag, "Carrying a Big Carrot: Linking Multilateral Disarmament and Development Assistance," *Columbia Law Review*, vol. 91 (June 1991), pp. 993–1059; and Daniel Tropper, "Arms Cuts for Land," *Jerusalem Report*, January 16, 1992, p. 40. Among these diverse incentive programs, the arms-for-debt swap is likely to be the least expensive; it is cheaper to forgive unserviceable debts than to raise new capital.

4. See Carl Connetta, Charles Knight, and Lutz Unterseher, "Towards Defensive Restructuring in the Middle East," *Bulletin of Peace Proposals*, vol. 22 (1991), pp. 115–34; and John D. Steinbruner, "The Consequences of the Gulf War," *Brookings Review*, vol. 9 (Spring 1991), pp. 6–13. A broad framework encompassing such new arms control proposals is presented in Ashton B. Carter, William J. Perry, and John D. Steinbruner, *A New Concept of Cooperative Security* (Brookings, 1992).

5. Edgard H. Habib, *International Petroleum Outlook* (Washington: WEFA Group, June 30, 1992).

6. Also known as Nasruddin Khoja. Many of the same stories that are told about Nasruddin or Juha are also attributed to Rabbi Nachman of Bratislava.

Index

Adeli, Mohammad Hossein, 63
Aid transfers among Arab states, 11–12
Akins, James, 69
Algeria, 12, 25, 32, 45, 46, 50
Arab-Israeli peace process, 3, 4; arms control and, 4; nuclear weapons and, 43–44
Arms control in Middle East: Arab-Israeli peace process and, 4; asymmetrical arms control arrangements, 43; "balance of power" perspective on, 5; collective security arrangements and, 54–55; CSCME proposal, 45; debt reduction and (*see* Arms-for-debt proposal); economic incentives, 9–10, 23–24, 40, 50–51; foreign powers, role of, 80–81; future prospects, 81–82; incentive programs, 80; Iran and, 61–66; Israel and, 57–61; military security and, 79; multilateral talks, 4; nuclear nonproliferation, 41–44; obstacles, 7, 70–72; opportunities following Gulf War, 2; petroleum factor, 8–10; Saudi Arabia and, 66–72; suppliers' negotiations, 4–5, 75–76; supply-side controls, 79–80; U.S. policy on, 2–3, 75
Arms-for-debt proposal: arms control negotiations and, 50–51; creditors' interest in, 46–47 "gearing ratio" issue, 49–50; IMF support for, 47, 49; Israel and, 60–61; Jordanian proposal, 45–46; success, chances of, 55; synergistic nature, 50

Arms race in Middle East: causes, 5–6; countries responsible, 56, 57; economic obstacles, 72–73; expenditures on, 1–2, 3, 8, 9; future prospects, 81–82; international arms trade and, 7–8; missile proliferation, 6–7, 39; opportunity costs, 78–79; petroleum factor, 8–10; political aspects of U.S. arms sales, 76–77; results, 1; Saudi arms buildup, 20, 67–69, 71–72, 73; social investment and, 26; U.S. role, 7–8, 73–77, 80–81; "vicious circle" pattern, 6
Asad, Hafiz al-, 37
Asymmetrical arms control arrangements, 43
'Azm, Sadiq al-, 30

Bahrain, 52, 53, 72
Baker, James A., III, 1, 54
"Balance of power" perspective on arms control, 5
Banca Nazionale del Lavoro, 42
Barak, Gen. Ehud, 60
Battlefield performace of Arab armies, 30–31
Bishara, Abdallah, 71
Borders in Middle East, 5–6
Bush, George, 2, 3, 41, 74–75

Camdessus, Michel, 47, 49
Chemical weapons, 43
Cheney, Richard, 71
China, 7, 35; arms sales in Middle East, 7–8; Iran, arms sales to, 6, 64; suppliers' arms control negotiations, 4–5

Collective security arrangements:
arms control and, 54–55;
functioning, 54; obstacles, 66–68,
69–70; pan-Arab programs, 51–
53; West-Arab alliance, 53
Commonwealth of Independent
States, 35, 64
Condor II missiles, 7
Conference on Security and
Cooperation in Europe (CSCE), 45
Conference on Security and
Cooperation in the
Mediterranean, 45
Conference on Security and
Cooperation in the Middle East
(CSCME), 45
Conscription of military personnel, 73
Cooperative security, 80
Czechoslovakia, 33, 35

Damascus Declaration, 52, 70
Debt-for-nature swaps, 46–47
Debt problem, 12–13, 34. *See also*
Arms-for-debt proposal; *specific
countries*
Demilitarization in Middle East:
battlefield performace of Arab
armies and, 30–31; economic
incentives, 26, 28; economizing
strategies, 39–40; international
pressures and, 35; Jordanian
program, 44–45; military elites'
views on, 29–32; popular support
for, 25, 37; Syrian example, 32–
38; trend toward, 38. *See also*
Arms control in Middle East

Economic situation of Middle East:
aid transfers among Arab states,
11–12; arms control and, 9–10,
23–24, 40, 50–51; demilitarization and, 28; Gulf War and, 14–
23; military elites' concerns
about, 29–30; petroleum exports
and, 8–10, 11–12. *See also* Arms
race in Middle East; Debt
problem; *specific countries*
Egypt, 28, 30, 46, 47; agricultural
programs, 29; arms race,
responsibility for, 56, 57; arms
reductions, 57; collective security

arrangements, 52; debt problem,
12; food imports, 12; Gulf War,
impact of, 23; Gulf War military
role, 20, 31; military industries,
28; military strength, 1; missile
proliferation, 7; nuclear
nonproliferation, 41, 43; officer
corps, 32

Fahd, king of Saudi Arabia, 67, 68
Food imports, 12, 29
France, 47, 53; arms sales in
Middle East, 7–8; suppliers' arms
control negotiations, 4–5
Front Islamique du Salut (FIS), 25

Gates, Robert, 64
Gorbachev, Mikhail, 35
Great Britain. *See* United Kingdom
Gulf Cooperation Council (GCC),
52, 54, 62
Gulf War, 1; aftermath, 3–4; Arab
forces, performance of, 30–31;
Arab states outside Gulf, impact
on, 23; arms control hopes and,
2; casualties, 16; cost of
damages, 19, 20; economic
motives, 14; Iraq, impact on, 14–
17; Jordan, impact on, 17–19;
labor exchange system and, 17–
19; Saudi Arabia, impact on, 19–
21; Saudi intellectual quarantine
and, 67; technological warfare,
68–69

Hoagland, Jim, 2
Human development in Arab
states, 26, 27; military spending
and, 28–29, 47
Hussein, Saddam, 1, 13, 14, 30
Hussein I, king of Jordan, 45
Hussein rockets, 6

Incentive programs for arms
control, 80
International Monetary Fund
(IMF), 19, 46, 47, 49
Iran: arms control policy, 65–66;
arms race, responsibility for, 56,
57; economic development, focus
on, 62–64; economic problems,

61–62; military buildup after *1988*, 64–65; missile proliferation, 6; nuclear weapons, acquisition of, 42. *See also* Iran-Iraq War

Iran-Iraq War, 30; impact on Iran, 62; impact on Iraq, 13; "War of the Cities," 6

Iraq, 28, 29; agricultural irrigation system, 16; arms race, responsibility for, 56, 57; arms reductions, 57; economic problems (pre–Gulf War), 13–14; Gulf War, economic impact of, 14–17; inflation, 16; invasion of Kuwait, 14; military and social spending, 26; military strength, 1; missile proliferation, 6, 7; nuclear nonproliferation, 43; nuclear weapons program, 41–42; officer corps, 32; population growth, 12; UN embargo against, 15. *See also* Iran-Iraq War

Islamist movements, 25

Israel: arms-for-debt proposal and, 60–61; arms race, responsibility for, 56, 57; debt problem, 58–59; economic incentives for arms control, 58–59, 60–61; Iraqi reactor, attack on, 41; military doctrine, 7, 57–58; military spending debates, 59–60; military strength, 1; missile proliferation, 7; nuclear capabilities, 42, 43; Soviet immigrants, 58–59, 60; U.S. arms sales to, 74–75. *See also* Arab-Israeli peace process

Italy, 45

Jericho II missiles, 7

Jordan, 8; arms-for-debt proposal, 45–46; CSCME proposal, 45; debt problem, 12, 46; demilitarization measures, 44–45; food imports, 12; Gulf War, economic impact of, 17–19; labor crisis, 17–18; peace dividend, hope for, 28; population growth, 12

Juha, Sheikh, 81–82

Kazakhstan, 42

Kissinger, Henry, 29

Korea, North, 6, 33, 35, 64

Kuwait: aid transfers to Arab states, 12; arms purchases following Gulf War, 71, 72–73, 74; collective security arrangements, 52, 53; food imports, 12; guestworkers, expulsion of, 18; Gulf War military role, 31; Iraq, relations with (pre–Gulf War), 14; Iraq's invasion of, 14; recovery from Gulf War, 21, 23; U.S. military presence, 53

Labor exchange system, 17–19

Lebanon, 4

Libya, 6, 12, 45

Mauritania, 12, 45, 50

Military elites, demilitarization and, 29–32

Military manpower of Arab states, 52, 53

Military security: arms control, relation to, 79; paramount importance of, 78

Military spending as development issue, 28–29, 47

Missile proliferation, 6–7, 39

Mitterrand, François, 47

M-9 missiles, 7

Moda'i, Yitzhak, 59

Morocco, 12, 20, 45, 46

Mubarak, Hosni, 41

"New world order," 2

Nuclear nonproliferation, 41–44

Oil, economics of, 8–10, 11–12

Oman, 12, 52, 53

Operation Desert Storm. *See* Gulf War

Organization of Petroleum Exporting Countries (OPEC), 11

O'Sullivan, Edmund, 19

Pakistan, 42

Palestinians, 43–44

Peres, Shimon, 59
Perle, Richard, 5
Petroleum, economics of, 8–10, 11–12
Population growth, 12
Preston, Lewis, 49
Professional military forces, 39–40

Qatar, 12, 52

Rabin, Yitzhak, 4
Rafsanjani, Ali Akbar Hashemi, 63, 64
Russia, 35

Sa'id, Nuri al-, 52
Saudi Arabia: agricultural programs, 29; aid transfers to Arab states, 12; arms purchases following Gulf War, 20, 67- 69, 71–72, 73, 74; arms race, responsibility for, 56, 57; borrowing by, 21; collective security arrangements and, 52, 54, 66–68, 69–70; food imports, 12; foreign policy, 69; guestworkers, expulsion of, 17–18; Gulf War, economic impact of, 19–21; Gulf War military role, 31; intellectual quarantine, 66–67; missile proliferation, 7; as obstacle to arms control, 70–72; officer corps, 32; population growth, 12; U.S. military presence, 70
Scud-B missiles, 6
Shamir, Yitzhak, 4
Shavit missiles, 7
Social investment, arms race and, 26
Soviet immigrants in Israel, 58–59, 60
Soviet Union: arms sales in Middle East, 7–8; Gulf War, 20; suppliers' arms control negotiations, 4–5; Syria's debt to, 37; Syrian arms buildup, 33, 35
Sudan, 12, 32, 46, 50

Supply-side arms control, 79–80; negotiations on, 4–5, 75–76
Syria, 4, 6, 8, 28, 29, 30; arms purchases, 33, 35; arms race, responsibility for, 56, 57; arms reductions, 57; collective security arrangements, 52; debt problem, 12, 35, 37; Gulf War military role, 20, 31; Gulf War windfall, 33; military strength, 1; military vs. social spending, 26, 35–38; missile proliferation, 7; nuclear nonproliferation, 43; officer corps, 32; population growth, 12

Tunisia, 45, 46
Turkey, 20

United Arab Emirates, 12, 14, 52, 53
United Kingdom, 53; arms sales in Middle East, 7–8; Gulf War, 20; suppliers' arms control negotiations, 4–5
United Nations, 15
United States, 29, 47; arms control policy, 2–3, 41, 75; arms race in Middle East, influence on, 7–8, 73–77, 80–81; "balance of power" perspective on arms control, 5; Gulf states' dependence on U.S. security umbrella, 76; Gulf War, 20, 68–69; military presence in Middle East, 53, 70; nuclear nonproliferation, 41; political aspects of arms sales to Arab states, 76–77; suppliers' arms control negotiations, 4–5; Syrian arms buildup, 35

Violence, Middle Eastern propensity for, 8–9, 10

World Bank, 12, 35, 49

Yemen, 8, 12, 47, 50